Vaught's Practical Character Reader

BY

L. A. VAUGHT
EDITOR OF HUMAN FACULTY

"This was the noblest Roman of them all;
His life was gentle, and the ELEMENTS
So MIXED in him, that Nature might stand up
And say to all the world: 'This was a man!'"
—SHAKESPEARE.

CHICAGO
L. A. VAUGHT, PUBLISHER
130 DEARBORN STREET
1902

LANE LIBRARY

M. A. DONOHUE & COMPANY
PRINTERS AND BINDERS
407-429 DEARBORN STREET
CHICAGO

PREFACE.

The purpose of this book is to acquaint all with the **elements** of human nature and enable them to read these elements in all men, women and children in all countries.

At least fifty thousand careful examinations have been made to prove the truthfulness of the nature and location of these elements.

More than a million observations have been made to confirm the examinations.

Therefore, it is given the world to be depended upon.

Taken in its entirety it is absolutely reliable.

Its facts can be completely demonstrated by all who will take the unprejudiced pains to do so.

It is ready for use.

It is practical.

Use it.

L. A. VAUGHT

INTRODUCTION.

Human character is the same as human nature in its last analysis. Human nature is composed of elements that are unchangeable in their nature and the same the world over. At least forty-two of these elements are now known. Individual character is a particular combination of these elements in which some lead or predominate.

To read character, then, is to understand these elements and determine their individual and relative strength in men, women and children. This can be done. Heads, faces and bodies tell the story.

To Handle Human Nature
To Educate Human Nature
To Train Human Nature
To Govern Human Nature
To Perfect Human Nature

DEFINITELY
SAFELY AND
SUCCESSFULLY

Is to clearly understand the

ELEMENTS
OF
HUMAN NATURE

	Language.
	Number.
	Order.
	Color.
	Weight.
	Size.
	Form.
	Individuality.
	Eventuality.
THE	Locality.
	Time.
	Tune.
	Alimentiveness.
	Acquisitiveness.
	Constructiveness.
ELEMENTS	Mirthfulness.
	Causality.
	Comparison.
	Human Nature.
of	Suavity.
	Imitation.
	Ideality.
	Sublimity.
	Spirituality.
HUMAN	Benevolence.
	Hope.
	Veneration.
	Firmness.
	Conscientiousness.
	Cautiousness.
NATURE	Secretiveness.
	Destructiveness.
	Combativeness.
	Vitativeness.
	Amativeness.
	Parental Love.
	Conjugality.
	Inhabitiveness.
	Friendship.
	Continuity.
	Approbativeness.
	Self-esteem.

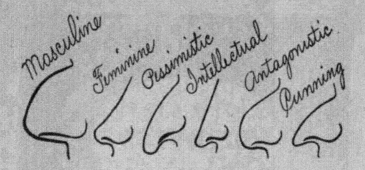

Observe for yourself.

THE HEART OF CHARACTER.

The very heart of human character is the faculty of Conscientiousness. It is the **core**. No character is **sound** that is not strong here. An apple is not sound that is **rotten** at the **core**. A human body is not strong with a **weak backbone**.

Neither is a soul **morally** strong with a weak faculty of Conscientiousness.

It is the **nuecleolis** of **substantial** character. The heart of anything is the most important part about it. To improve human character **specifically** is to develop this faculty. All other methods **are necessarily empirical, general and indefinite.**

HIGH TIME TO BE DEFINITE.

It is time to be definite in education.

It is time to be definite iin the study of man.

It is time to be definite in talking, writing or preaching about human questions—HIGH TIME.

To be definite is to understand the **elements** of human nature.

POSITIVELY
HONEST.

Make a sharp contrast between this and the opposite.
He that hath eyes to see, let him see. Here is a good
head from a back view. What a wonderful difference
between this and the other!

HONESTY.

Honesty is almost wholly made up of the element
of Conscientiousness alone. To be positively honest
is to have a strong degree of this faculty, Self-esteem
and Firmness. These three faculties, when predominant in the mental constitution of anyone will make
him wholly reliable.

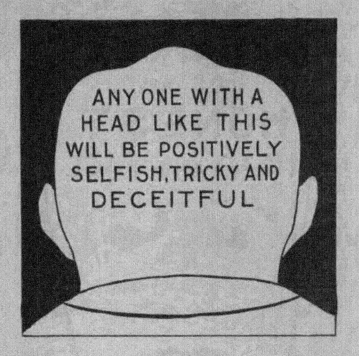

ANY ONE WITH A
HEAD LIKE THIS
WILL BE POSITIVELY
SELFISH, TRICKY AND
DECEITFUL

Here is an outline of a head that we want all men, women and children to perfectly fix in their minds. Make use of every opportunity you have of looking at heads from a back view.

DECEITFULNESS.

The elements of human nature that make people deceitful are Approbativeness, Amativeness, Secretiveness, Alimentiveness, Acquisitiveness and Vitativeness. When these are very strong and Conscientiousness, Friendship, Benevolence, Self-esteem and Veneration weak, one will take the cake for deceitfulness.

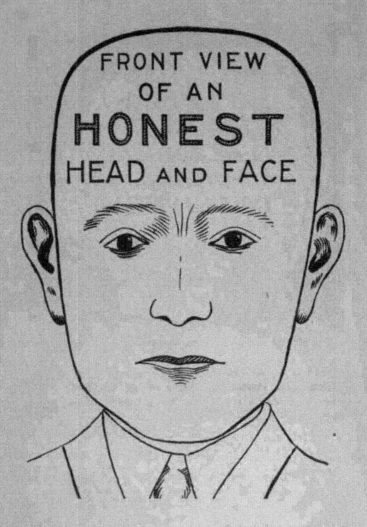

FRONT VIEW
OF AN
HONEST
HEAD AND FACE

It will pay all to remember the shape of this head and face.

**Here is the exact location from a side view of the most
reliable faculty of the human mind—Conscientiousness.**

UNDERHANDEDNESS.

Those who take underhanded ways of doing selfish
things may be known by having predominant elements
of Secretiveness, Approbativeness, Amativeness and
Acquisitiveness.

With Conscientiousness, Self-esteem and Combativeness weak they will take to underhanded ways very
soon after birth.

Just observe or examine closely enough to learn
if the four first named faculties are in the lead and
you may rest absolutely assured that the party is
underhanded in his ways whatever he may claim to
the contrary.

HOSPITALITY.

The elements of hospitality are Friendship, Benevolence and Approbativeness.

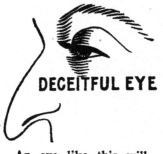

An eye like this will represent a character that is positively deceitful. Why not use your own eyes and not be deceived by such?

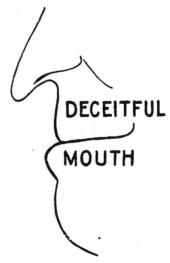

One with a mouth like this can be very agreeable and still have the most selfish ax to grind.

Study this chin young ladies and gentlemen and do not depend too much upon the constancy of anyone with a similar chin.

Clearly remember this shape and apply it.

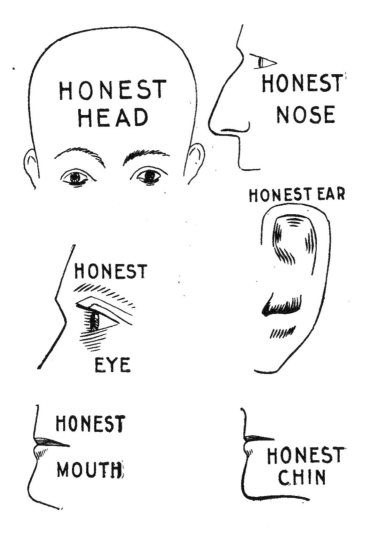

DECEITFUL EAR

Keep your eyes open in dealing with people with ears like this.

INSINCERITY.

The insincere man or woman is without enough Conscientiousness Self-esteem, Friendship, Conjugality, Parental Love, Veneration, Benevolence and Combativeness to be courageous, self-respectful, honest and frank. Then some of his selfish faculties will resort to insincere words, protestations, actions and promises. Be sure that one has a strong degree of Conscientiousness, Self-esteem, Friendship and Benevolence, before you depend upon his promises.

JUDGE THOMAS McINTYRE COOLEY.

A Standard of honesty.

Here is a head and face that truly represent natural, inherent honesty. Specially study his face, and particularly his eyes.

Gustave Kindt.
Alias French Gus, Burglar and Tool-maker.

ALL THE SIGNS OF HONESTY.

An open eye.

An eye that is steady.

An eye that can look **you** in the eye without an effort.

An eye that does not look furtively nor out of the corners at you.

An eye that is not restless.

Upper eyelids that are inclined to form angles.

Perpendicular wrinkles between the brows above the base of the nose.

A strong, straight-lined, clear-cut nose.

A firm, steady mouth.

A square chin.

A well-formed ear that is somewhat square at the top and bottom.

Straight lines anywhere in the face.

Open hands.

Square finger tips.

A walk in which the heel strikes the floor first.

A tendency to throw the toes outward instead of inward in walking.

Lack of pretension.

A disposition to **consider** any question.

Frankness of manner.

Disposition to **trust others.**

Lack of suspicion.

A candid, straightforward manner of statement.

A voice that is clear, natural and direct in its tone.

More important than all alse: a well-developed **upper** backhead and particularly a high rather square and **convex** back tophead.

CONCENTRATION.

The **power** of **voluntary** concentration is to be found in the elments of Firmness, Self-esteem, Continuity and Combativeness. With these four elements and Individuality one can concentrate his intellectual faculties on any subject he chooses and as long as he desires.

Very simple when one understands it.

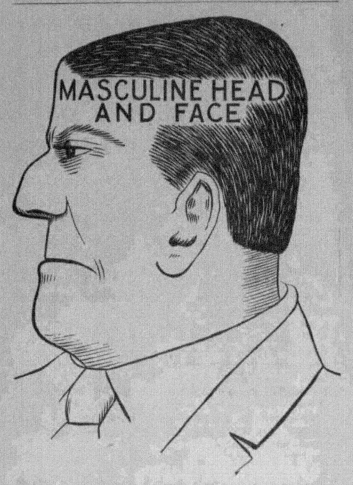

Here is a masculine head and face, made so by the masculine faculties of the mind. Masculinity is inherent in certain faculties. When these are in the lead they not only give a masculine nature but form the masculine head, face and body.

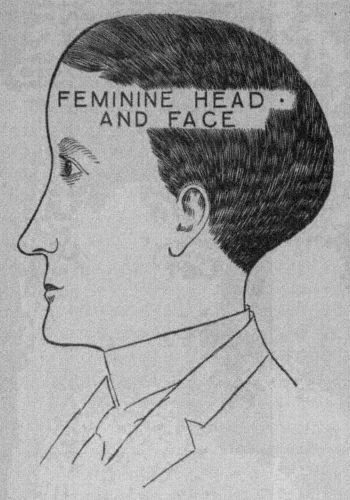

FEMININE HEAD
AND FACE

Why is this head and face the opposite of the masculine? Because the feminine faculties are predominant. There is a great vital truth right here.

First ascertain by observation and examination if the feminine faculties named are predominant and the rest can be taken absolutely for granted. It is better to understand and begin with **causes** than to simply notice effects. The causes of all kinds of heads, faces and bodies that are **natural** are the **elements** of human nature.

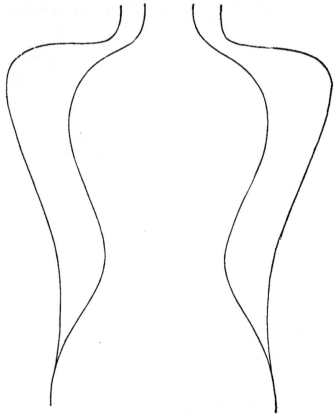

A true illustration of positive masculine and feminine forms.

MASCULINITY.

One is masculine by virtue of certain faculties. Masculinity is made up of certain faculties or mind elements just as certainly as the United States is made up of states and territories. These are: Destructiveness, Combativeness, Firmness, Self-esteem, Amativeness, Causality, Number and Constructiveness. When these eight elements of human nature predominate in one's mental composition he will have a masculine mind, voice, head, face and body. Human Nature builds the body. Certain elements of human nature when in the lead, build a body on masculine lines. The head will be square in front, high in the crown, nearly perpendicular in the back and the face will be broad nose large and broad, the upper lip straight, the mouth large, stiff and cut in straight lines, the chin large, thick and square, the jaw square, neck large and shoulders square.

This will be true, whether man or woman.

FEMININITY.

While certain primary faculties make one masculine other faculties just as certainly make one feminine. To be feminine in disposition, head, face and body is to have the faculties of Benevolence, Parental Love, Approbativeness, Cautiousness, Conjugality, Comparison, Spirituality, Human Nature and Eventuality in the lead in the formation of one's mind. The head will be narrow from ear to ear, the backhead round with the upper portion fullest, the frontal part of the tophead high and broad, the forehead nicely curved and fullest in the center beginning at the base of the nose. The nose will be small and curved, the eyes round, the mouth small and beautifully curved and the chin and neck small. The shoulders will be curved, the hips broad and the body as a whole more round or curved than square.

A GENUINE MOTHER.

We affirm in the most absolute manner that words can be used that mother love is located exactly where this backhead projects most. To be a true, natural mother is to have this faculty highly developed. Young men, fix this picture in your minds.

MOTHER LOVE.

Mother love is nothing more nor less than the faculty of Parental Love. It all comes from this one faculty.

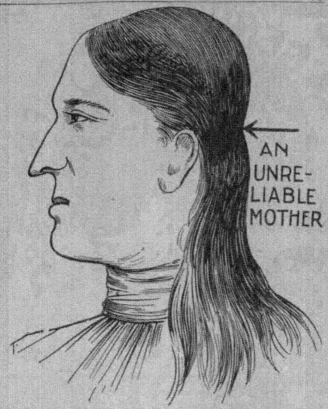

AN UNRE-LIABLE MOTHER

This is a striking illustration.   It will pay all to remember this head formation and especially all men who would select wives who will make good mothers.

SLOVENLINESS.

Why is one slovenly?   Because his faculties of Ideality, Order, Self-esteem and Approbativeness are weak. Positively nothing more true.

ANOTHER KIND OF CRYING.

There are selfish children who seem to cry but do not. They use the cry as a means to an end.   This should not be termed crying, but calling, bawling, howling, screeching.

AN UNRELIABLE FATHER

We emphatically advise women to distinctly bear in mind that all men with heads shaped like this are unreliable as fathers.

Young ladies, indelibly fix this shape of head in your memories. Any man who will make a natural, kind and true husband will have a head in outline from a side view like this.

PREJUDICE.

Prejudice is composed of Friendship, Parental Love, Conjugality, Inhabitiveness, Approbativeness, Veneration and Destructiveness. These elements when in the lead will give one a strong feeling **for** something or some-
'y and **against** the opposite.

AN UNRELIABLE HUSBAND

The reason this man is an unreliable husband is because he is very weak in Conjugality and Parental Love and exceedingly strong in Amativeness. Young ladies, beware of such men as husbands.

BIGAMY.

Bigamy comes directly from Amativeness. Conscientiousness is weak and Secretiveness large.

POLYGAMY.

Polygamy is an amalgamation of Amativeness, Spirituality and Veneration. Strange, but perfectly true.

LOVE.

What is love? How may it surely be determined? Love is made up of three individual sentiments: Friendship, Conjugality and Amativeness. Therefore it may be understood, measured and analyzed. There can be no love between the sexes without some degree of these three primary sentiments or elements of mind. They are located in the backhead. This is the first place to look for love. Go to **head** quarters. But one may have much more of one of these elements of love than another. Here is the "rub." This can be determined by proceeding to read character in the following way: When the base of the backhead is larger and fuller than the upper part, passional or amatory love is in the lead. This kind of love is physical and not lasting. The eyes will have thick lids and not be very open; the lips will be large, coarse and particularly developed in the center of each; the chin will be large and thick **downward.**

When Conjugality is in the lead, the upper part of the backhead will be the largest and fullest. This will give a round, full, symmetrical form to the entire backhead. This faculty never flirts, while Amativeness does. Conjugality is devoted to **one.** It likes the company of **one.** It desires marriage, while Amativeness desires a good time and is indifferent about marriage. When Conjugality is in the lead of Amativeness in one's love nature, the eyes will be open and candid, the lips refined, nicely curved and not very thick nor full in the center; the chin will be comparatively thin and the neck not large.

When Friendship is in the lead of the other two love sentiments, the upper part of the backhead will be decidedly the fullest, especially in width. The lips will be refined and with small lines running across them. Out from the corners of the lips there will probably be two or three curved lines which indicate active, hospitable friendship.

When the three elements of love are all strong the backhead will be very round and full.

ALL THE SIGNS OF LOVE.

Rather large, rainbow, rosy lips.

A well-developed chin.

A tender, open and sparkling eye.

A pleasant, warm, affectionate tone of voice.

A warm grasp of the hand.

A disposition to cling.

More important than all alse, a **full round backhead.**

HOW TO PICK OUT A GOOD CHILD.

To pick out a good child be sure that the **upper** backhead is very strongly developed and also the **whole** tophead. When these two sections of the head are very highly developed there are **innate** in the child those elements that will love home, parents, friends, morals and religion. If these two regions of the head are poorly developed the reverse will be true. Then if the head is not very broad from ear to ear the child will have no positive tendencies toward vice, crime and meanness.

IMPRESSIBILITY.

The elements of impressibility are Approbativeness, Spirituality,. Cautiousness, Benevolence, Veneration, Ideality, Sublimity, Hope, Conscientiousness, Amativeness, Conjugality, Friendship, Parental Love and Inhabitiveness.

Approbativeness is impressible to praise,

Spirituality to mysticism,

Cautiousness to fear,

Benevolence to suffering,

Veneration to fear of God,

Ideality to beauty,

Sublimity to grandeur,

Hope to prospect,

Conscientiousness to duty,

Amativeness to sex,

Conjugality to marriage,

Parental Love to children,

Friendship to friendliness,

Inhabitiveness to patriotism.

If all of these faculties were predominant in man or woman, either would be acutely impressible.

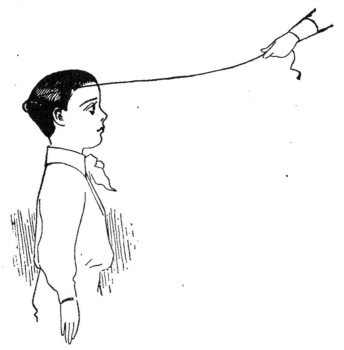

A pointed illustration of how to lead children who have strong affections represented by a full backhead.

AFFECTION.

There are only five elements of affection in the whole human soul. These are: Friendship, Conjugality, Parental Love, Amativeness and Inhabitiveness. They are all located in the backhead and fill it out when large.

EASILY INFLUENCED.

Any man, woman or child is easily influenced who has Approbativeness, Benevolence, Friendship and Amativeness in a strong degree and Self-esteem, Firmness, Conscientiousness and Combativeness weak. A volume could not make this more plain.

HOW TO LEAD CHILDREN.

There is no rule by which children can be handled—the composite make-up of the human mind makes null and void the universal practicality of a rule. The very best way is to understand children—to understand them part by part or elementally. Each child is composed of fundamental elements. Each inherits these in different degrees of strength. A very accurate knowledge of the individual and relative strength of these faculties in a child is the only reliable basis of leading children properly. Without this knowledge, parents and teachers have to experiment with children and then never truly know whether they are proceeding in the proper way or not. What we mean by the proper way is that way that will best fit the child for future Self-control, Success, Health and Happiness.

Any child can be led if fully known. Every child has some strong faculties or at least some that are stronger than others. Paradoxical as it may seem, in one sense these are the child's weaknesses. He will give attention through them. By means of these strong faculties he may be led into a higher channel. The above illustration shows how one kind of boy may be easily led. The ring (as it were) to which the cord is attached is put through his backhead—the region of his affections. When a boy has a round, full backhead like this he can be led easily by means of his affections. He will respond quickly to friendly approaches. He likes to be loved and petted. He will be interested, too, in pets of some kind—a dog, pony, parrot or pig.

By means of these he can be led into the study of natural history and science if properly handled.

Parents and teachers should know what heads mean. They should know the faculties that are located in the different parts of the head. Very much safer would be their guidance and successful their government of children.

One may be strong intellectually and socially idiotic, as distinctly represented by this head and face.

HYPNOTIC POWER.

What constitutes hypnotic power? It is made up of Self-esteem, Firmness, Combativeness, Secretiveness, Spirituality, Human Nature, Individuality, and Destructiveness. These give great self-confidence, will, force, positiveness, coolness, secrecy, tact, mysteriousness and concentration, which constitute hypnotic power, just as certainly as eight ones make eight.

JULIA WARD HOWE.

Author of the "Battle Hymn of the Republic," etc., etc.
A sincere face, of the thinking, listening type. The
faculty of Individuality is negative.

PROF. A. GRAHAM BELL.

A remarkable degree of the faculty of Individuality, the center of observation.

We wish to emphasize in the most absolute way the fact that so far as a human being is concerned all danger lies in these two faculties. They are easily located and should be understood by every man, woman and child. Be on guard against the danger in such men and women.

PUGNACITY.

Pugnacity comes directly from Combativeness. Then if Destructiveness, Approbativeness and Amativeness are also very strong one will be positively pugnacious.

Anyone with a head like this is dangerous in a vicious sense because Destructiveness is very strong and Cautiousness and Conscientiousness weak.

THE TWO DANGEROUS ELEMENTS OF HUMAN NATURE.

There are only two **dangerous** elements in human nature. We mean just what we say—there are only two dangerous elements in human nature. Then when you wish to determine whether there is anything dangerous in a man, woman or child, examine his or her head and ascertain if Destructiveness or Amativeness is strong. No one of the other elements can hurt you or anyone else. Without these two there could be no seduction, enticing into vice or leading astray on one hand, nor any anger, hatred, revenge, rage, violence, vindictiveness, poisoning or murdering on the other. Fix this truth in your intellect and then look for the development of these two faculties. If they are strong there will be possible danger always, and when Conscientiousness, Benevolence and Friendship are weak, positive danger. Nothing known by man is more absolutely true than this.

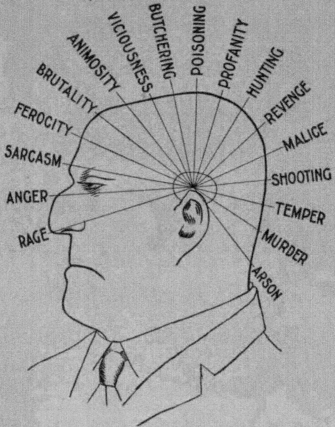

The above illustration speaks volumes for itself. Destructiveness is the center of all the characteristics named here.

PROFANITY.

There is only one faculty in the human mind that can give one any desire to really swear, and this is De-

structiveness. Children may be led into using profane words by the faculties of Imitation and Approbativeness, but when one really d——s any one or
anything he uses Destructiveness. Children with Destructiveness predominant take to swearing like a duck
to water. Those who have this faculty weak and large
Benevolence and Veneration are horrified by profanity.
Anyone with large Destructiveness will have a strong
tendency to swear.

Without any modification of words, we say that no
one can feel any degree of revenge without the faculty
of Destructiveness. Here is the very heart of it.

REVENGE.

There is only one element of human nature whereby any man, woman or child, of any tribe, nationality or race can feel revengeful. This is the element called Destructiveness. All of the other elements may be cheated, beaten or robbed and manifest no revenge. Why? Because they are not constituted that way. Look, then, for a positive faculty of Destructiveness if you wish to know whether there is that in one that will hold a grudge and resolve to get even   Ill-will, hatred, malice, revenge—all must come through the element of Destructiveness. How? By means of some other element being hurt or imposed upon. Cheat Acquisitiveness and it will try to get revenge through Destructiveness. Offend Approbativeness and it will do the same. Hurt Parental Love by hurting a child and it will fly to Destructiveness and the two will cry for revenge. All the other faculties have to go to Destructiveness if they mete out revenge for being unjustly dealt with.

ALL THE SIGNS OF ENERGY.

A broad head from ear to ear.
A large and broad Roman nose.
A stiff upper lip.
A high crown of the head.
Dense, wiry hair.
No surplus flesh.
A bright, snappy eye.
A large, square chin.
A square jaw.
Rather large bones.
Square shoulders.
Large cheeks.

More than all else, strong faculties of Destructiveness, Combativeness, Firmness, Approbativeness and Amativeness.

FRIVOLITY.

A frivolous disposition comes from a dominant degree of Amativeness, Approbativeness and Mirthfulness.

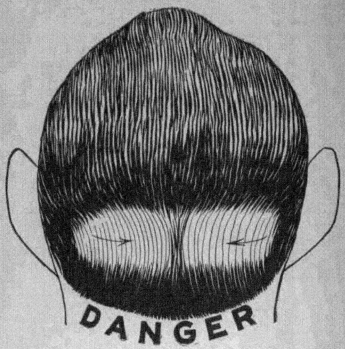

Anyone with a head like the above is dangerous because Conscientiousness is weak and Amativeness very strong. In an immoral sense this man is positively dangerous.

BRUTALITY.

How may one be brutal?

By means of large Destructiveness and some other selfish faculty like Alimentiveness, Acquisitiveness, Amativeness or Approbativeness.

Alimentiveness or Destructiveness will make one brutal when hungry or intoxicated.

Acquisitiveness and Destuctiveness will make one brutal in the getting and holding of money or property.

Amativeness and Destructiveness will make one brutal in the gratification of lust.

Approbativeness and Destructiveness will make one brutal in rivalry and jealousy.

In all such case one must remember that Benevolence, Conscientiousness, Friendship, Conjugality and Parental Love are not strongly developed. Always look or examine to see how strong these faculties are.

Notice the straightness of the upper lids and how hard they press down upon the balls. This means possible cruelty.

This is a true picture of a gross, sensual chin.

WHAT IS SAVAGEISM?

Savageism is a predominating degree of Destructiveness with small Benevolence.

MILITARY NATURE.

The composition of military nature is Combativeness, Destructiveness and Approbativeness. The first to give a love of combat, the second of shooting and the third of fame and victory.

MOODS.

The human mind is so many sided that one can show a great variety of moods. A particular mood is a particular faculty in a high or predominating state of action.

A mirthful mood is the element of Mirthfulness leading all the others in action.

A surly mood is Destructiveness leading. A friendly mood is friendship in the lead of all others in action.

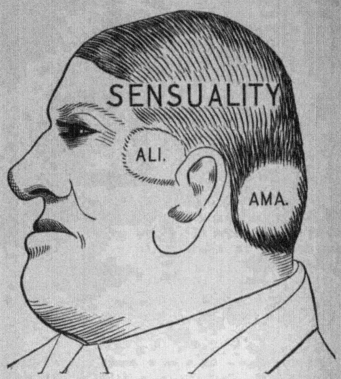

Sensuality is wholly made up of two elements—Alimentiveness and Amativeness. This illustration shows the location of these and when very strong in head and face. Remember the picture and apply it to others.

SENSUALITY.

Sensuality can be gotten right at. It can come from no other source than two fundamental elements of the mind, to wit: Alimentiveness and Amativeness. The first gives gustatory and the second amatory pleasure. To be an all round sensualist, then, is to simply live in or under these two faculties. They are as easily located as the ear and nose and almost as easily seen.

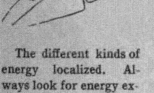

The different kinds of energy localized. Always look for energy exactly where it is located.

A striking comparison. Some have less ability than they think they have and some a great deal more.

ENERGY.

The two primary and exact sources of energy are Combativeness and Destructiveness. These two elements are inherently active. That is, they love action or effort without any attachments or other axes to grind. Destructiveness is the fundamental element of all energy that comes under the head of forceful. Combativeness covers all energy that contends. The two together, like everything of a forceful, struggling, wrestling, pushing, driving, destroying, overcoming kind, whether it be a desk that is hard to open, a game of football, a stump in the field or a mountain that has to be tunneled or removed. This is their pleasure.

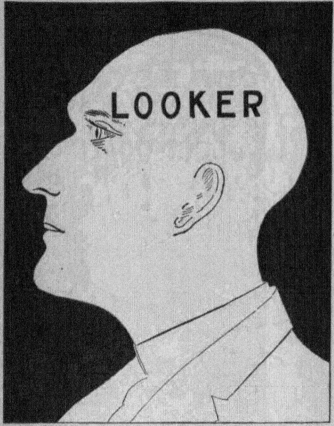

LOOKER

All should fix this outline in their minds and compare it with the opposite.

THE VISUAL STUDENT.

The student who is mentally organized to learn chiefly by vision has the mind elements of Individuality, Form, Size, Locality, Color and Order predominant. One may have perfect eyes and be weak in these faculties, and learn very poorly by vision. This is a great fact for educators.

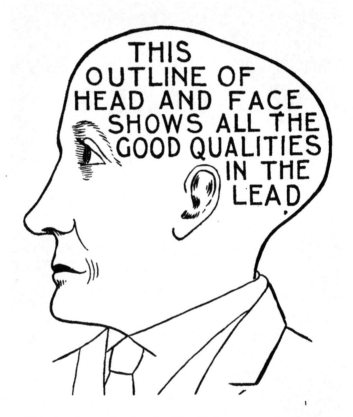

This head speaks for itself. It is an emphatic fact.

AWKWARDNESS.

Why is one awkward? Because he has predominating faculties of Approbativeness, Destructiveness,
Cautiousness and weak faculties of Human Nature,
Individuality, Weight, Time, Amativeness, Combativeness and Self-esteem.

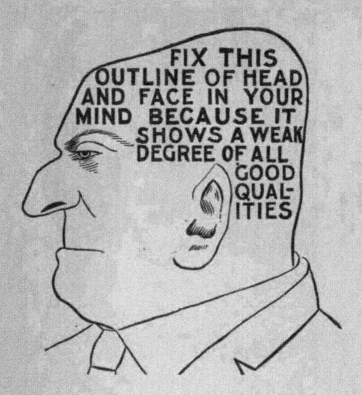

FIX THIS OUTLINE OF HEAD AND FACE IN YOUR MIND BECAUSE IT SHOWS A WEAK DEGREE OF ALL GOOD QUALITIES

Fix this outline to stay fixed in your mind, because it will pay you to do so.

GREED.

The primary elements of greed are Alimentiveness and Acquisitiveness. Suppose these two elements are very strong and Benevolence, Conscientiousness and Friendship very weak. Then one will be an out and out pig.

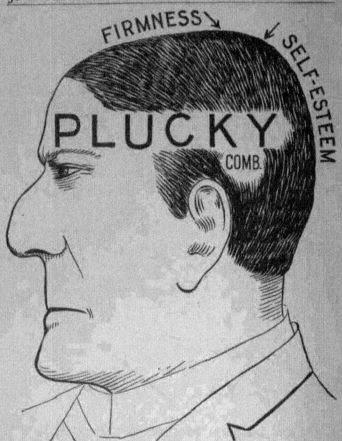

Pluck is a fact. Here is an illustration that explains the fundamental elements of it.

PLUCK.

The elemental ingredients of pluck are Combativeness, Firmness, Destructiveness, Self-esteem. The chief one is Combativeness. If moral pluck, Conscientiousness is added. Add any other element to the four primary elements and you get a particular kind of pluck.

THE TWO PRIMARY CAUSES OF
NERVOUSNESS

Here we hit the nail right on the head.   All mental nervousness and nearly all physical nervousness springs directly from these two elements.   This is a great fact for all who are thus afflicted and for all teachers, parents, physicians and psychologists.

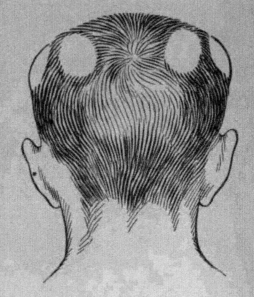

The two elements of fear and nervousness from a back view.

BLUSHING.

To blush is to have enough of the element of Approbativeness to make one fear some kind of ridicule or
criticism. Without this faculty no one can blush. If
Self-esteem is weak and Conscientiousness, Cautiousness and Veneration strong one will be a great blusher.

CASTE.

Caste comes from only two elements of human nature;
Approbativeness and Self-esteem, but chiefly from the
former. It is a mixture of vanity and self-importance,
and wholly without merit. There may be talent and
character connected with it, but the feeling itself is
wholly the product of two selfish elements.

Here is a striking illustration of the wants, accumulations and expressions of a single faculty—Approbativeness.

VANITY.

The center of human vanity is the faculty or element called Approbativeness. To be vain is to be flattered through this faculty. When this faculty is very strong one is subject to some kind of flattery and can easily be made vain. No other element of human nature cares for praise. It is easy to locate this faculty in the head. It causes the head to be held to one side.

It makes the voice affected. It curls the mustache upward. It does the same with the corners of the lips. It shows the upper teeth when praised, and minces the walk. When the crown of the head is high and the center of it where Self-esteem is located is low, this faculty will be very active. Then if the faculty of human nature is weak there will be great susceptibility to flattery.

JUST PRESS THE RIGHT BUTTON.
Whenever you wish to get the attention
Of Jones or Smith, O'Connor or Dutton,
Don't whistle nor sing, nor profane things mention:
Just walk up to the head and press the right button.

HEAD WORK.
To do head work a good degree of two mind elements is absolutely necessary. These are Comparison and Causality All should bear this in mind. Never se-
nyone to do head work unless he has a good
of these two elements. To do constructive
ork, add Constructiveness.

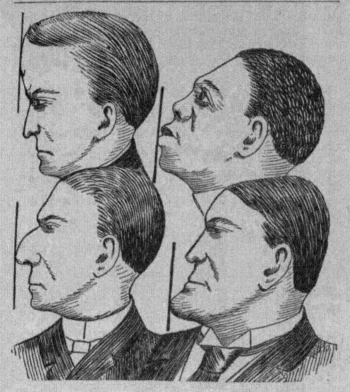

WHICH TOUCHES THE LINE?

The above illustration is a very instructive one. It will enable our readers to get at the predominant characteristics of anyone at a glance when they fully understand it, and when the individual to be read has one or more predominant faculties.

That part of the face or head that projects most forward (if normal) tells what part of the mind is predominant. Special development of parts of head or face means special strength of certain faculties.

When the upper forehead is the most pronounced in development the reasoning or thinking faculties

(Causality and Comparison) of the mind are predominant. Such a person will be an abstract, absent-minded thinker. Is very likely to be an ideal theorist. He may be a profound philosopher but not very practical.

When the nose gets to the line first there is a very different character because other faculties are predominant in the mental constitution. In such cases some of the courageous, selfish, forceful faculties predominate. In a word, energetic force is predominant in the individual. We do not say, however, that such a person will necessarily be a very strong character in every particular. He may have no very strong faculties, but when this part of the face does predominate the faculties that go with it do also.

Combativeness and Destructiveness are the two faculties that correspond with the convex anterior projection of the bridge of the nose, while if the nose is thick at the same time, Acquisitiveness and perhaps Secretiveness are also strong. Such people have some kind of active energy, and when the nose is broad, selfish energy.

There is a very different set of faculties predominant when the lips touch the perpendicular line first. Then the appetites and social sentiments predominate. Such are impulsive, sentimental, sensual and often voluptuous. They make emotional speakers and are almost wholly governed by impulse.

Where the chin is the most forward feature, tenacity of life is predominant, and if the chin is square and long, persistence is also very strong. Where the chin is not so square and long but thick in muscular covering and fleshy, sexual passion is stronger than persistence.

When these four divisions of the face are all strongly developed or when they show a positive convex form, there will be a strong character intellectually, executively, vitally and sentimentally.

Here we have a well balanced or level head.

What is a level head?   In common parlance it is the way of saying that one has a well-balanced **mind**.   What a well-balanced mind is, is no easy thing to explain. An incomplete explanation would be this: One with Human Nature, Causality, Individuality, Number, Conscientiousness, Acquisitiveness, Firmness, Combativeness and Self-esteem, predominant.

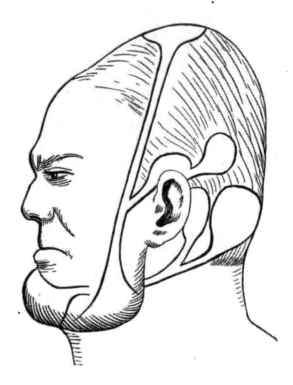

Here can be seen the faculties of the mind that build the lower jaw—to wit: Amativeness, Combativeness, Destructiveness and Firmness.

PUGILISM.

The mind elements that give a love of pugilism are Combativeness, Destructiveness, Amativeness and Approbativeness. Just as certainly as these four faculties are **predominant** in **anyone** he will be fond of baseball, football, athletics and boxing.

The principal reason that one has a long face with all the features turning downward as indicated in this illustration, is because those faculties of the mind that ought to fill out his top head and make it round and full are deficient. A roof-shaped head is pessimistic.

DISAGREEABLENESS.

The make-up of Disagreeableness is Destructiveness, Firmness, Approbativeness, Secretiveness and Alimentiveness. When these are strong and the five agreeable faculties are weak, one is very disagreeable generally. Such a person will tease, combat, boast, criticise and delight in worrying others.

A GREAT PROBLEM SOLVED.
THE REASON WHY OF HUMAN DIVERSITY.

The number of Human Beings that may exist without two being alike.

A MATHEMATICAL SOLUTION.

According to Permutation, the forty-two individual faculties of which the human mind is composed may combine in 2,810,012,235,505,759,797,086,285,212,489,023,-129,540,768,000,000,000 different ways, which will account for all the diversity of the human family in the past, at present and for a few hundred million years in the future.

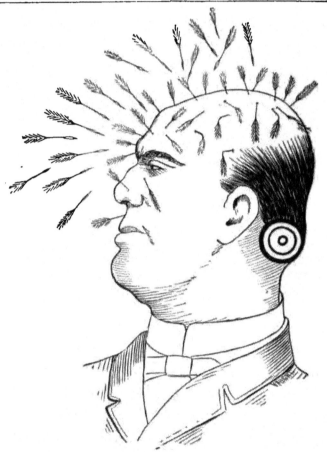

This picture shows how moral reformers shoot at random at vice. They do not know the location of vice, and therefore shoot wildly. Not a single arrow has hit the bull's eye.

THE CENTER OF THE SOCIAL EVIL.

The social evil is a fact. Many good and learned people are trying to check, modify or suppress it. Their intentions are good. They shoot at it with tongue and pen. That is, they suppose they shoot at it. They shoot, but, unfortunately, they do not shoot any more definitely at it than if they stepped out of their houses upon a dark night when the moon was down, electric lights out, and shot into space in the hope of hitting a burglar. Why don't they draw a bead on it? Answer: They do not know the location of it. They do not know the nature of it. They do not know the source of it. They do not know that it is a single element of the mind. They do not know when nor where to commence to correct it. They ought to know. They can know.

They can know exactly. They can know very soon after the babe is born. They can, if they will, learn the location of the faculty in the brain. Observe the illustration. Not one of the marksmen has hit the "bull's-eye." Every shot has missed. What a deplorable waste of time, energy and arrows!

They have hit the intellect, which is in front, the moral faculties, which are in the tophead, pride and vanity, which are in the back crown of the head, but not a single one has even come close to the exact source of the evil. They have not even crippled it. How could they cripple it till they hit it? How can they hit it till they know where it is?

It is located in the little brain directly back of the two bony prominences that may be found and felt behind the ears. When very strong in child, woman or man this region will be decidedly full or convex in form. It is immediately below a fissure that runs horizontally above it, and partly separates the little brain from the big brain, or, in other words, the cerebellum from the cerebrum.

Its name is Amativeness.

We now have it "spotted."

We know where to look for it.

No longer is it necessary to shoot at random. We can now see it so distinctly and individually that we can hit it every time if we are good shots.

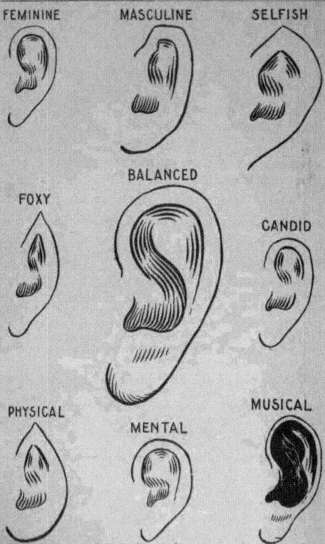

FEMININE   MASCULINE   SELFISH

FOXY   BALANCED   CANDID

PHYSICAL   MENTAL   MUSICAL

Just look for yourself.

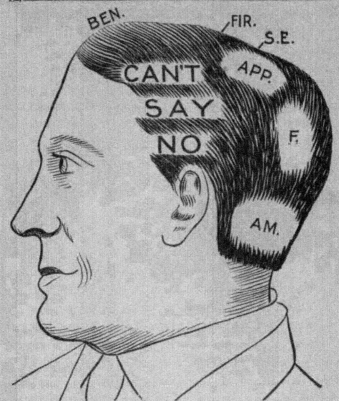

Get all of this. Many are somewhat organized like the above. Here is a complete and pointed explanation of the reason one cannot say no.

IMPULSIVENESS.

What makes people impulsive? Intellect is not impulsive. There is no impulse in a single intellectual faculty. There is no impulse in Firmness or Self-esteem. There is impulse in Cautiousness, Destructiveness, Benevolence, Friendship, Approbativeness, Parental Love, Combativeness, Amativeness, Alimentiveness, Inhabitiveness, Veneration, Acquisitiveness, Ideality

Mirthfulness, Hope and Sublimity. To be impulsive then is to let one or more of these elements act without regulation. Impulses start in these faculties. If they are much stronger than Self-esteem, Firmness, Conscientiousness, Human Nature and Causality in anyone he will be impulsive. Simply ascertain by a close examination of the head by sight or hand or both if the five last named faculties are predominant or not and you can tell whether one belongs to the impulsive class or not.

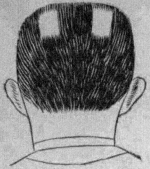 

| This shows the location of the sensitive faculty of Approbativeness from a back view. It is one that all should exactly locate. | Men, women and children with such shaped heads as this are fitful. They are deficient in application, perseverance, decision and resolute, unchangeable will. |

CHANGEABLENESS.

A positive disposition to change comes from Locality, Ideality, Constructiveness and Destructiveness, with weak Veneration, Firmness, Self-esteem, Continuity and Inhabitiveness.

RATTLES.

To get a case of rattles is to let the element of Approbativeness get unduly excited. This faculty causes stage fright, blushing and embarrassment. No other element has the power to rattle.

PERSONAL MAGNETISM.

To be magnetic is to have very strong faculties of Friendship, Amativeness, Alimentiveness, Combativeness, Human Nature, Benevolence, Mirthfulness, Firmness, Causality, Language and Comparison.

Amativeness and Alimentiveness furnish the vital magnetism. Friendship, Benevolence and Mirthfulness the social magnetism. Combativeness and Firmness the courageous magnetism. Language, Causality Comparison and Human Nature the intellectual magnetism. The three that have by far more to do in making one magnetic than all others are Friendship, Combativeness and Amativeness. These three faculties when very strong will make anyone magnetic. James G. Blaine had Friendship. General Phil Sheridan, Combativeness, and Brigham Young, Amativeness. Unite these in a predominant degree in one man and you have the "secret" of personal magnetism.

PHYSICAL CHARMS.

Physical charms are the product of strong, healthy faculties of Amativeness, Alimentiveness and Parental Love with a fair degree of Combativeness and Destructiveness.

THE ARGUMENTATIVE DISPOSITION.

The fundamental and specific source of the argumentative disposition is Combativeness. This faculty likes to contend for **contention's sake**. United with Language it will contend with **words**. If Approbativeness is added to these two, there will be a **wordy** contention for victory. If Firmness is added there will be a **persistent** spirit of contention. If Causality is added to these, there will be a wordy, ambitious, persistent, logical contention. Destructiveness will add force and bitterness to the contention and may be **blows** or **pistols**. If Secretiveness, Human Nature and Constructiveness are also strong and Conscientiousness weak the contender will resort to strategy, ingenuity and cunning in his contentions. In this way the argumentative disposition may be gotten at fully and fundamentally.

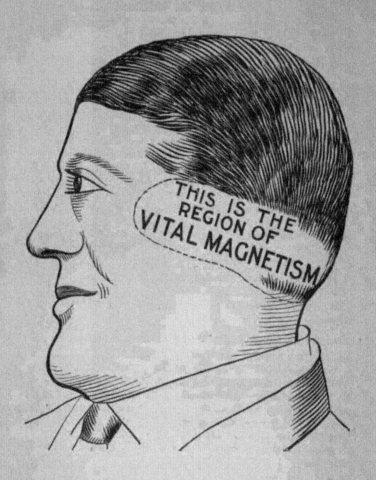

A very valuable fact is illustrated right here. Vital
magnetism wholly comes from this region. Not an
iota comes from any other faculty of the mind or part
f the brain.

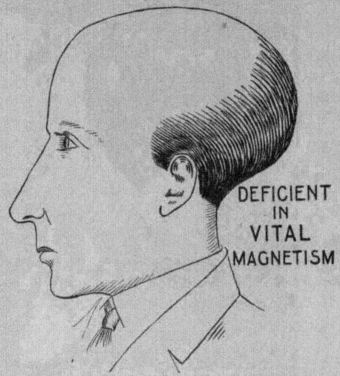

DEFICIENT
IN
VITAL
MAGNETISM

Anyone can demonstrate the truthfulness of the above by mere observation.

LATENT VITALITY.

If a child has a strong development of Alimentiveness, Vitativeness and Amativeness it will have much **latent** vitality. It may be puny and not grow well for a while but if rightly cared for will surprise the parents and friends by growing into a strong man or woman. In such cases there has been arrested development by sickness of mother, prenatal influences or improper food. Always go to the brain for **certainty** in any kind of character reading.

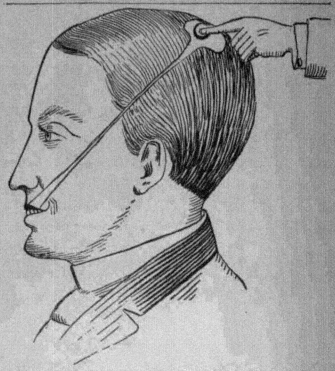

This is another illustration of the fact that if you press the right button (excite the right faculty) you will get the right response. Touch approbativeness and you will raise the upper lip.

DISPOSITION TO CROW.

The "crowing" faculty is Approbativeness. None other. Others will give force to the crowing, but not any of the desire. If Destructiveness is strong and Benevolence and Conscientiousness weak, one will "rub it in."

RELIGIOUSNESS.

The fundamental religious elements are Spirituality and Veneration. Their first assistants are Hope, Benevolence and Conscientiousness. Without the two first no religious organizations could have ever been.

ELISHA GRAY.

A scientific form of head.   Great perceptive faculties.

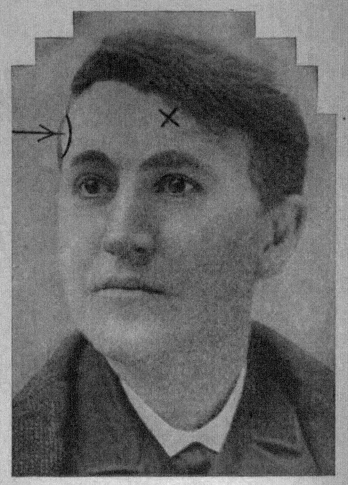

THE KEYNOTE OF EDISON'S GENIUS.

Genius may be understood—clearly understood.
It may be clearly understood because it is **always** and
wholly composed of elemental faculties. These facul-

ties can be understood and **measured** in all men, women and children.

If there is any particular kind of genius there is always a very high development of those fundamental faculties that **constitute** the particular kind of genius. Mechanical genius is made of mental elements that by their very nature cannot constitute literary, musical or commercial genius.

Thomas A. Edison's genius is well known as the **inventive**. It is not commercial or musical.

The "keynote" of it is the elemental faculty of Constructiveness. His portrait overwhelmingly indicates this. That great convex development of the middle side temples is the result of a very strong degree of the faculty of Constructiveness which has its seat here and develops its two organs (one in each hemisphere) till they positively determine the **formation** of the external skull.

The second element of his inventive genius is Causality the logical thinking faculty. These two faculties are the two most original faculties of the forty-two facultied soul.

His eyes and head show an active faculty of Spirituality also which gives him a consciousness of the **undiscovered** and faith in his efforts.

He has a great development of those faculties that the constitution of the human mind **necessitates** to possess the very original inventive genius that he has so remarkably displayed.

CURIOSITY.

Curiosity is the product of Individuality, Causality, Spirituality, Constructiveness, Approbativeness, Secretiveness and Amativeness. Individuality gives a desire to see a thing; Causality to understand it; Spirituality to marvel at it; Constructiveness to understand how it is constructed; Approbativeness to get it before somebody else does; Secretiveness to suspiciously pry into it and Amativeness to revel in the scandal of it. When these faculties are predominant in one he is a veritable curiosity seeker, looker and investigator.

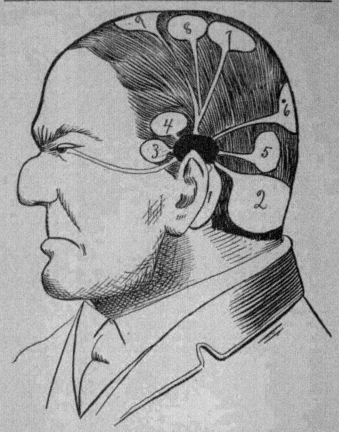

Destructiveness is the center of human temper. The nine other faculties that stir it up principally are Vitativeness, Amativeness, Alimentiveness, Acquisitiveness, Conjugality, Inhabitiveness, Approbativeness, Conscientiousness and Veneration.

TEMPER.

Human temper has a beginning. In one sense, we may say that there is a temper faculty; yet this is not exactly right, because the function of the faculty from which temper springs is not exactly one of temper. This much may be said, however, there is a faculty without which no one can feel any temper.

This faculty is Destructiveness. Its function is not simply to destroy; it is dynamic force. It is, also, the only faculty by means of which one can feel anger, malice and the tendency to crush or destroy. In itself it will not result in a manifestation of this kind. It is only when some other faculty is hurt that Destructiveness becomes angry.

PRETENSION.

The elements of pretension are Approbativeness, Alimentiveness, Acquisitiveness, Amativeness. There are no other elements that can give any desire to pretend. To successfully pretend is to have in addition to the above named, Secretiveness and Human Nature. Not to be pretentious is to have Conscientiousness and Self-esteem predominant.

DIAGNOSE YOUR OWN CASE.

Make use of the following
definite self-knowledge.

If you are nervous your faculties of Cautiousness and Approbativeness are dominating the rest of you.

If you cannot say no to one of the same sex, your Friendship, Approbativeness and Benevolence are relatively too strong.

If you cannot say no to the opposite sex, it is Amativeness, Approbativeness and Benevolence.

If you cannot say no to children, it is Parental Love Benevolence and Approbativeness that prevent you.

If you get rattled easily your faculties of Self-esteem and Firmness are not large enough.

If you get the "blues" easily, your Self-esteem, Combativeness, Firmness, Spirituality and Hope are too weak.

If you are irritable, Approbativeness, Destructiveness and Combativeness have got the upper hand of you.

If you are absent-minded, Individuality, Locality, Human Nature and Cautiousness are not large enough to keep in front. Just as surely as you keep these faculties in **front** you will never become absent-minded.

If you fail to remember names, Language, Self-esteem, Approbativeness and Tune are not so strong as they ought to be to make you give particular attention to them. People with these faculties strong always give attention to names and therefore remember them.

If you are broad between the eyes, however, you can remember names by writing them down and fixing them in your faculty of Form.

If you hesitate or stammer in speech, you are deficient in Self-esteem, Firmness and Combativeness and should immediately cultivate these three faculties by the most courageous and self-respectful action.

If you borrow trouble, the **trouble with you** is too much Cautiousness and Approbativeness.

If you are tempted to steal because you love somebody's else property or watermelons, it is because Acquisitiveness and Alimentiveness are pretty strong in your mental make-up.

If you are inclined to hold a grudge, remember that it is only because your Destructiveness is larger than your Benevolence and Conscientiousness.

If you think you are going to die and don't, your Vitativeness and Cautiousness have command of you.

If you believe that "every man has his price" your own Conscientiousness is very weak.

If you imagine that someone has slighted you, your Approbativeness is much too strong for its antidote, Self-esteem.

If you won't sleep in room thirteen at a hotel, your faculty of Spirituality is too strong for your Comparison and Causality.

If you cannot keep your mouth shut, your Firmness, Self-esteem and Secretiveness are too weak. If these three faculties were predominant in you, your mouth would shut up like a clam.

If you forget dates your faculties of Time and Number are weak.

If you are impatient your faculties of Self-esteem, Firmness, Conscientiousness, Causality, Spirituality, Hope and Veneration are not strong enough. These, when dominant in one, give him the patience of Job.

If you are not attractive, your faculties of Friendship, Amativeness, Ideality, Benevolence and Order are not as strong as they should be. Cultivate them.

IRRITABILITY.

Irritability starts in the faculty or element of Approbativeness. This is the sensitive faculty. It has a great deal to do with making a sensitive, nervous system. Now if Destructiveness and Combativeness are also large one will possess the chief elements of irritability. This is just as true as one and two make three. Let these three faculties positively predominate over all the others and **anyone** will be positively irritable. Simply ascertain if these faculties predominate in one and you will find an irritable man, woman or child with absolute certainty.

This illustration represents the manifold productions of a single faculty—Mirthfulness. It chiefly makes the clown, the comedian, the wit and the humorist.

LOVE OF MISCHIEF.

Love of mischief springs directly from the element of Mirthfulness. When it is very strong. Veneration weak and Secretiveness, Destructiveness and Human Nature large, one will run over in fun-loving mischief and the playing of prank on others in school and out of

The above illustration shows the location of two mind elements that a child, even, can see. It is almost inconceivable that anyone cannot see the formation of head that these two faculties, when dominant, produce. They stand out in bold relief upon millions of men, women and children. Two such dangerous faculties should be as quickly seen as the nose and ears. They are Destructiveness and Amativeness.

FLIRTATION.

Why does one want to flirt? Because of Amativeness and Approbativeness, and these only. If these two faculties are very strong in one, he or she will have a strong tendency to flirt. If they predominate, one will be an out and out flirt. Both faculties are very easily understood, and may be easily measured in others. Look directly for these two faculties for flirtation.

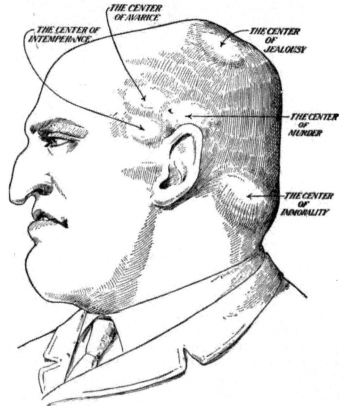

Here are the locations of five elements that it will pay you to thoroughly learn. When predominant they build the kind of face seen upon this head.

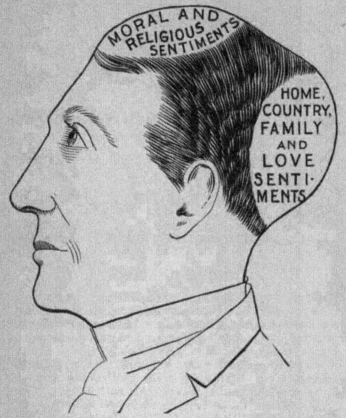

Always look for sentiment in these two regions of the head. There are no other sentiments and no other places to look for them. We say this with absolute certainty.

DOMESTIC NATURE.

Domestic nature is made up of Parental Love, Conjugality, Inhabitiveness, Alimentiveness and Acquisitiveness. If these are predominant in any woman she will be positive in domestic nature.

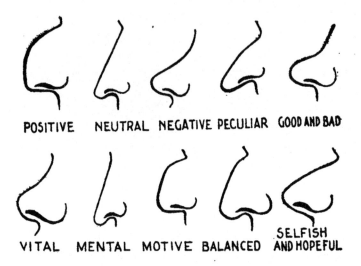

POSITIVE   NEUTRAL NEGATIVE PECULIAR GOOD AND BAD

VITAL   MENTAL   MOTIVE   BALANCED   SELFISH AND HOPEFUL

WHERE TO LOOK.

If you wanted to know whether a man had a nose or not wouid you look somewhere in general? Would you look for it on his backhead? In looking for mental faculties you should be just as definite as in looking for the nose. For instance, in looking for the faculty of anger always look where it is naturally and always located. This is just above the tips of the ears on the sides of the head. It is never anywhere else. One ought to know just as certainly where to look for mental elements or faculties as he knows where to look for the nose.

PESSIMISM.

The faculties that make the pessimist are Cautiousness, Secretiveness, Destructiveness, Alimentiveness, Amativeness and Approbativeness with weak Hope, Spirituality, Benevolence, Veneration, Conscientiousness, Mirthfulness, Self-esteem, Combativeness and Ideality.

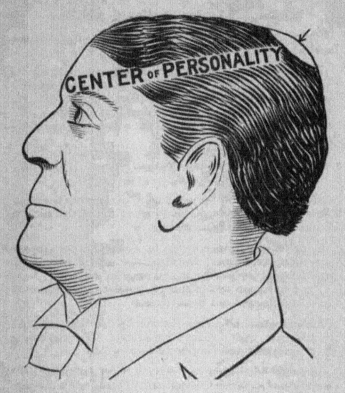

To be strongly individualized and have a distinct personality is to have a predominant faculty of Self-esteem, as indicated in the above picture.

INDIVIDUALISM.

The mental elements that make one a positive individualist are Self-esteem, Combativeness, Vitativeness, Firmness and Individuality. These make him believe in himself, depend upon himself, educate himself and positively individualize himself.

SPECIFIC KINDS OF CHILD NATURE.

Any distinct kind of child nature is made up of distinct faculties.

Vicious child nature has large Destructiveness for its center, with Combativeness and Amativeness usually large and Benevolence and Conscientiousness negative. Destructiveness is the central element of viciousness. No one can be vicious in a brutal sense without a strong degree of this faculty.

Stubborn child nature is made up principally of Firmness, Approbativeness and Combativeness. If this is of a very **forceful** kind, Destructiveness is added.

Sensitive child nature is made up of Approbativeness, Cautiousness, Benevolence and Veneration, with deficient Combativeness and Self-esteem.

Lying child nature is made up principally of Approbativeness, Sublimity, Spirituality and Secretiveness, with deficient Conscientiousness and Self-esteem.

The two essential elements of **moral** child nature are Conscientiousness and Benevolence.

Affectionate child nature is made up of Friendship and Amativeness, with deficient Self-esteem, Combativeness, Destructiveness and Firmness.

Studious child nature of the positive type is made up of Causality, Comparison, Eventuality, Ideality and Spirituality. These give a positive, inherent love of study. If Approbativeness and Conscientiousness are also large there will be an ambitious, conscientious love of study.

Playful child nature has its seat in Destructiveness with three special assistants—Mirthfulness, Amativeness and Combativeness. These four faculties predominant will make any child love games and all plays that are amusing.

Timid child nature is made up of Cautiousness, Vitativeness and Spirituality, without Combativeness and Self-esteem.

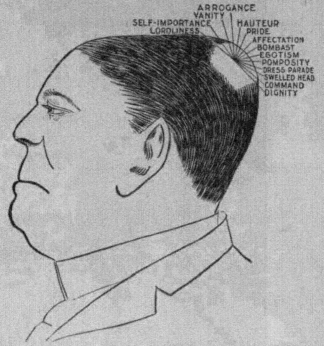

ARROGANCE
VANITY
SELF-IMPORTANCE   HAUTEUR
LORDLINESS   PRIDE
AFFECTATION
BOMBAST
EGOTISM
POMPOSITY
DRESS PARADE
SWELLED HEAD
COMMAND
DIGNITY

This illustration speaks for itself.

THE DOMINEERING DISPOSITION.

The disposition to domineer springs from the faculty of Approbativeness and Self-esteem; the former slightly stronger than the latter. Add to these two, strong Combativeness, Destructiveness and Firmness and you have the constituents of the domineering disposition.

Such made up people have an over-weening desire to boss. It does them a world of good to dictate what others shall do. They like to "rule the ranch" and when Conscientiousness and Benevolence are weak they will rule or ruin.

The five above named faculties constitute all of the human disposition to dominate, command, domineer, dictate, boss and rule. They are easily understood, easily located in the head, easily seen in the face, easily heard in the voice and all readers of this book should easily avoid such people hereafter.

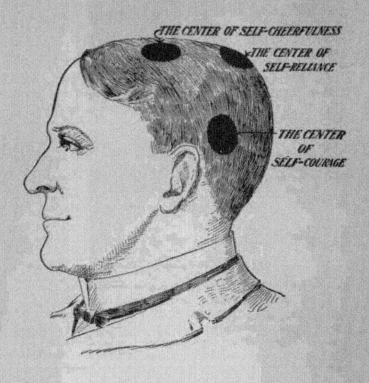

The faculties of everlasting self-reliant courage are indicated here. When these are predominant one is positively cheerful, and life is worth living to him. He never becomes despondent.

One with a head like this is clumsy because the perceptive faculties and self-confidence are weak. Look for yourself.

Those who have control of their appetites and feelings regulate their lips like the first outline; those who have not will have a position of the lips like the second.

STUBBORNNESS.

The chief element of stubbornness is Combativeness. It is this element of human nature in men, women and children that resists. No other element has resistance in its nature. The element of Firmness has **persistence** in it, but not resistance. If this is added to Firmness there will be **persistent resistance.** These two elements are therefore the chief elements of human stubbornness. The third one is Approbativeness. When the first two are strong, the third will add a strong dislike to giving up and make the stubbornness much more stubborn. When large Destructiveness is added to these three you have the make-up of stubbornness in all its glory.

The faculties that will tend to prevent these faculties from being unreasonably stubborn are Conscientiousness, Self-esteem, Benevolence and Causality.

This illustration shows the difference in position, at church during prayer, of two, one with positive and the other negative veneration. Notice the tophead of the gentleman.

GOODNESS.

Goodness is made up of six of the forty-two mind-elements, to wit: Benevolence, Conscientiousness, Veneration, Friendship, Conjugality and Parental Love. Without these one would have no desire whatever to do good to others in any way.

This skull shows a convex development of Destructiveness, Alimentiveness and Tune. An illustration of the external formation of a positive faculty.

This is the same skull. It shows the internal concavities that correspond with the external convexities of the other picture in this book. There is always a true correspondence between the normal development of faculties on the inside with the outside.

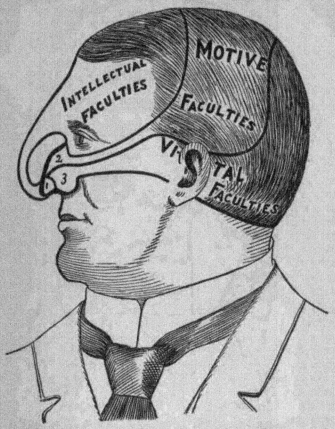

This illustration is full of meaning. It shows the relation between the faculties of the mind and a single factor of the face. Different faculties build different parts of the face. The vital faculties build the wings of the nose chiefly, and give it fleshy thickness. The motive faculties build the bone of the nose and make it Roman in form. The intellectual faculties chiefly build the tip to the nose. Take extreme cases of either and you will see for yourself.

Here is one who is the opposite of the materialistic.

PSYCHICAL SENSIBILITY.

There is a faculty that gives one a psychical tendency and sensibility. This is Spirituality. Coupled with Human Nature it gives not only psychical sensibility but the intuition to **interpret** mental impressions. The first **receives** and the second **interprets**.

This man is the opposite in mental make-up of the one who feels that he is spirit. Make a sharp comparison of the two heads.

MATERIALISTIC.

A materialist has weak Spirituality. Then, with strong Perceptive faculties, good Comparison, Causality, Alimentiveness and Amativeness he lives in the objective, concrete material, sensuous world and does not sense the Spiritual.

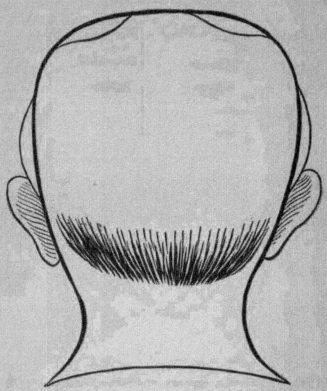

Study this picture. The difference between the heavy outline and the other is often all that stands between one and the penitentiary. The two dips on the tophead mean very weak Conscientiousness and the two convex formation on the sidehead mean very strong Secretiveness and Destructiveness. One makes a very good man and the other a possible criminal.

LONGEVITY.

The very heart of longevity is Vitativeness. Then if Alimentiveness and Amativeness are strong and under the control of the intellect and moral will, one will be naturally long lived. This may still be increased by large faculties of Hope, Combativeness, Self-esteem, Mirthfulness and Spirituality to give cheerfulness, self-control and patience. Longevity is largely a matter of self-control as well as of natural vitality.

GAMES.

Many love games like baseball, golf, tennis, billiards, etc., etc. Why? Because they have a strong development of certain constitutional elements. These are Combativeness, Approbativeness, Destructiveness, Amativeness, Weight, Size and Locality. Anywhere and everywhere when these faculties are strongly developed in men, women and children a strong love of games is the result. These faculties instinctively love playing, climbing, running, jumping, wrestling, racing and contesting. Combativeness sets the ball in motion. Any child with this faculty highly developed will intensely love some kind of game. Then if Approbativeness, the ambitious faculty, is strong, it will love the struggle for victory. Destructiveness loves motion, Weight loves balancing, Size measuring, Locality placing and Amativeness gives the masculine instinct of physical vigor as well as of muscular co-ordination so necessarv in playing all games.

FOLLY.

The chief ingredient of folly is Amativeness. The second Approbativeness and the third Alimentiveness.

SULLENNESS.

To be sullen is to use Approbativeness, Firmness, Combativeness and Destructiveness together with Approbativeness in the lead.

HUMANITARIANISM.

To be a humanitarian is to possess a very strong degree of Benevolence and Conscientiousness and strong Causality and Human Nature.

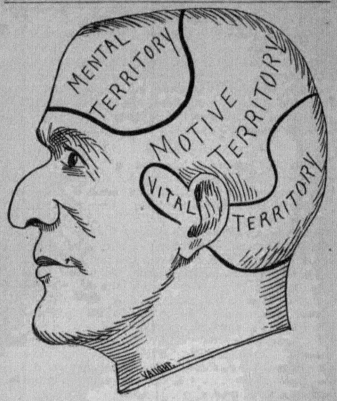

Temperament is a condition of the mind in which certain faculties predominate. The territory marked off here represents the location of the faculties that make the three temperaments.

LATENT TALENT.

When a young man or woman has the faculties of Causality, Constructiveness, Ideality, Sublimity and Spirituality strongly indicated in the formation of the brain and head and the head measures more than twenty-two inches in circumference, there will be considerable latent talent. Such will study better after seventeen years of age. Parents and teachers should bear this in mind.

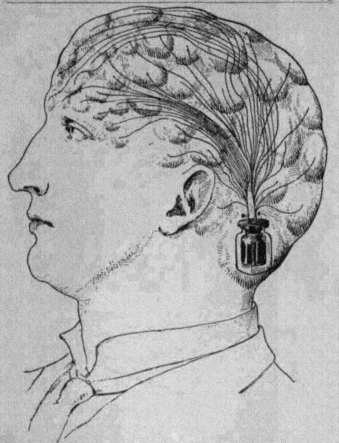

The vital dynamo of the brain is illustrated in the above picture. This is the faculty of Amativeness. It is a veritable dynamo of vital electricity.

CHEERFULNESS.

The fundamental elements of human cheerfulness are Hope, Mirthfulness, Spirituality, Self-esteem, Conscientiousness, Benevolence and Combativeness. Look for a strong development of these in the head and you will be sure of permanent cheerfulness.

CENTER OF IDEALISM

Here is an important fact. Those who are very broad exactly where the arrow points are inclined to all kinds of idealism.

IDEALISM.

center of Idealism is Ideality. When this faculty ant in the mind of anyone he will be some kind of idealist. If Form, Conjugality, Friendship, Benevolence, Conscientiousness and Amativeness are all strong he will idealize woman.

If Spirituality and Sublimity, in connection with Ideality, positively predominate over the other faculties one will be a positive idealist of the metaphysical type, like the Christian scientist, theosophist and psychic.

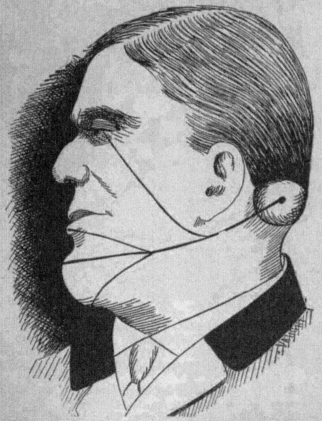

Here we have Amativeness with its facial poles and connections. It comes out in the face, in the eye, lip and chin.

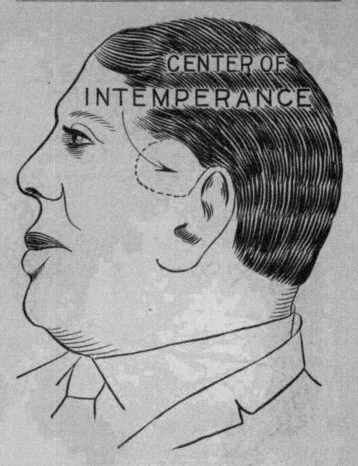

INTEMPERANCE.

Drinking and eating intemperately is specifically inherent in the faculty of Alimentiveness. By over eating and drinking one gets the whole digestive system in an abnormal condition which is perversion and becomes an intemperate habit. But the specific cause *is in* Alimentiveness.

The elements of the greatest human power are found in this combination. One with these faculties all dominant will be a powerful man vitally, physically, socially, intellectually, executively and morally.

EXECUTIVE TALENT.

This is made up of the following elements: Self-esteem, Firmness, Combativeness, Destructiveness, Human Nature, Comparison, Causality and Constructiveness. The latter four give tactful ability and the first the force to put it into practice.

This is Acquisitiveness grasping the "Almighty Dollar."

ACTIVITY.

The chief elements of activity are Combativeness, Destructiveness, Approbativeness and Firmness. These four elements in the lead of the others will make **anyone** very active.

DESIRES.

All desires spring from specific faculties.

The ambitional desire springs from the faculty of Approbativeness. The licentious desire from Amativeness. The desire for wealth comes from Acquisitiveness. The swearing desire comes from Destructiveness. The building desire comes from Constructiveness. The contentious desire comes from Combativeness. The desire for children comes from Parental Love. The desire for long life comes from Vitativeness. The desire for intemperate eating comes from Alimentiveness.

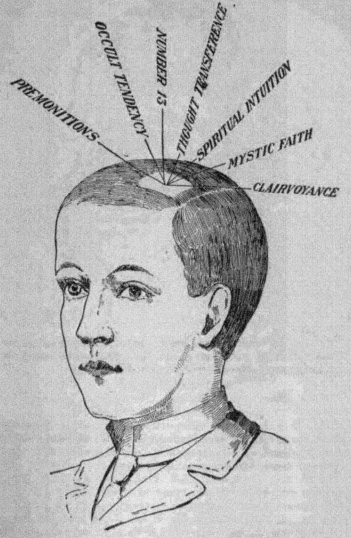

THE CENTER OF PSYCHICAL PHENOMENA.

The two faculties that make this man hold his head in this position and that give him the cunning, cautious expression are Secretiveness and Cautiousness.

RADICALISM.

To be radical in make-up is to have a predominant degree of Combativeness and Destructiveness with considerable Self-esteem, Approbativeness and Firmness. These will give a **positive tendency** toward radicalism of some kind. Then, if Veneration and Cautiousness are weak, there will be radical radicalism.

To tell the specific kind of radicalism one possesses pick out the strongest sentiment or other faculty. For instance, suppose the faculties developed to a strong degree that I have named. Then, if Acquisitiveness is a leader of the rest, one will be a radical speculator John W. Gates.

This picture is designed to represent the grasping miser or monopolist who knows how to make and take care of money. He has his own mental bank, as it were—Acquisitiveness.

AVARICE.

Avarice comes directly from Acquisitiveness. Then if Benevolence, Conscientiousness, Friendship, Conjugality, Parental Love and Approbativeness are weak it is the pronounced type.

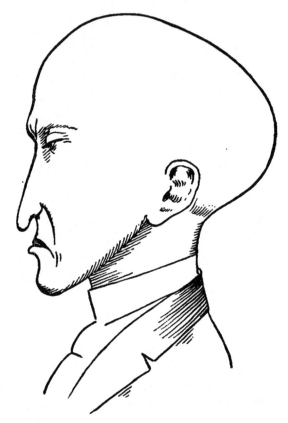

The minor keys or faculties predominate in this; notice the opposite.

The faculties that love music in the minor key are:

1. Cautiousness,
2. Approbativeness,
3. Veneration,
4. Benevolence,
5. Parental Love,
6. Conjugality,
7. Friendship,
8. Inhabitiveness,
9. Secretiveness,
10. Vitativeness.

Here is one with the major keys or faculties predominant.

The faculties that love music in the major key are:
1. Hope,
2. Mirthfulness,
3. Combativeness,
4. Self-esteem,
5. Amativeness,
6. Alimentiveness,
7. Ideality,
8. Sublimity,
9. Spirituality,
10. Firmness.

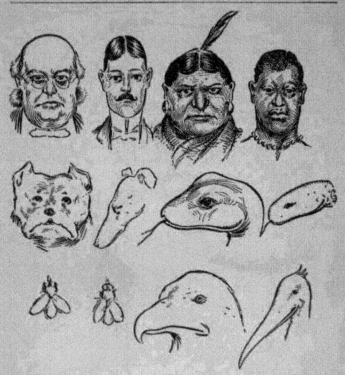

Here is a very positive demonstration. All very broad-headed humans, animals, birds, reptiles and flies are vicious. Very narrow-headed men and snakes are harmless.

THE CHARACTER OF BROAD HEADS.

Human faculties are not located just anywhere. They do not vary any more in location than do the eyes, nose, mouth and ears. We know where to look for the ears. We might know where to look for the savage, destructive, carnivorous elements of human nature just as well. They have a certain location. They are never found elsewhere. Their localization is in the temporal lobes of the brain and never elsewhere. Externally they cover the middle sidehead in which the tip of the ear is about the center. They therefore give width to the head directly through from one ear to the other. Broad heads mean something definite and fundamental. The fundamental faculties localized in the temporal lobes are Alimentiveness, Acquisitiveness, Destructiveness, Secretiveness, Combativeness and Vitativeness.

These six elemental faculties embrace in their nature all appetite, avarice, savagery, cannibalism, malice, venom, cunning, stealth, pugilism and tenacity of life. They constitute the predominant nature of the carnivora or that which determines a natural class of animals from other classes like the herbivora and granivora.

No animal could be carnivorous in nature without a dominant degree of these selfish elements. They are predominant in the eagle, lion, tiger, hawk, catfish, fox, hyena, rat, owl, butcher-bird, king-bird, shark, alligator, snapping turtle, wolf, swordfish, all poisonous snakes like the cobra, moccasin and rattlesnake and in all biting flies.

All of these have broad heads. In fact, any animal that has more brain in the temporal lobes than elsewhere will be vicious and carnivorous.

THE HUMAN NATURE OF FISHING.

Who has not felt that almost indescribable thrill that a "good bite" sends along the nerves from the hands to the brain? Where does it come from? What is it? It is a mixture of Cautiousness, Sublimity, Spirituality and Approbativeness. The bite jolts Cautiousness into nervous excitability, then Sublimity instantaneously imagines it to be little less than a whale in size. Spirituality adds that marvelous thrill that arises from all things unseen and Approbativeness is intensely excited for fear he will get loose and you will lose the glory of catching the biggest fish. Then if the fish is gamy, Combativeness and Destructiveness immensely enjoy the contest. Thus one has the love of fishing. Catching a mess for dinner is not fishing. Take away the faculties of Combativeness,

Destructiveness, Cautiousness, Sublimity, Approbativeness and Spirituality from one and the best fishing in
America will be insipid. These faculties do not give
the talent, however. This comes from the faculties
of Human Nature, Locality, Weight and Individuality.
Human Nature united with Sublimity and Locality
gives one that mysterious ability to tell good fishing
weather and places. A "born" fisherman must have
a positive faculty of Human Nature just as one who
loves the gamy contest of landing a big one must have
Combativeness.

HUMAN ATTRACTION.

The above illustration shows a very common attraction. It is a powerful magnet. Tens of thousands
are drawn that way as the magnet draws needles to it.
Why? Because they have very strong faculties of Destructiveness and Combativeness. Take these two fac-

ulties out of the mental constitution and the prize ring would absolutely drop out of human life.

No other faculties directly have any attraction for it whatever. There are two other faculties, however, that co-operate with Destructiveness and Combativeness, and indirectly give a tendency and ambition toward it. These are Amativeness and Approbativeness. Amativeness is a masculine sentiment. It is that faculty that makes the male animal want to whip all other males. It causes all male animals to contend. They contend for masculine supremacy or mastery of the herd. Two male animals who are strongly endowed with Amativeness will fight. In fact they will struggle to the death. This sexual sentiment stirs up Approbativeness, which desires victory. Approbativeness, therefore, in the sense of ambition, co-operates with Destructiveness and Combativeness in the pugilist.

Our object in illustrating human attraction is to familiarize all with the fundamental sources of everything human. We wish to still further make it stand out so plainly that it will be seen even in the babe. The mother ought to see all of the latent tendencies toward brutality, revenge and probably murder. The time to restrain these is in infancy. If parents cannot see what is inherent in the child, although latent, they may let it grow up and become positively dangerous to self and society. They will not see these things until they are strikingly illustrated. The readers of this book should use this illustration among their neighbors. They should get all of their neighbors interested in the localization of these lower selfish faculties.

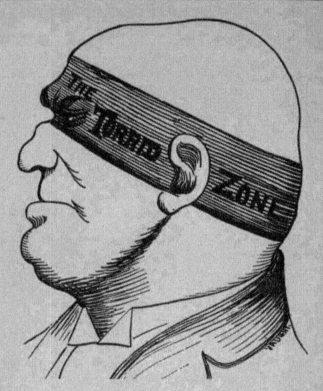

THE TORRID ZONE OF HUMAN NATURE.

There are zones of human nature more real by far than the imaginary climatic zones around this old world of ours. Yet how many school children know anything about the location of these human zones?

The above illustration shows the location of the torrid zone of character.

In this one the climate is exceedingly **hot**. The consequence is that the most violent storms are generated and sweep over the rest of the mental territory with terrific force. Hot fires of passion spring up and set the whole body aflame. Wars, murders, arsons, delirium tremens and mad houses are the fertile productions of this zone. Verily it is not far from H——. **It may be this is** the **veritable place.** It ought to be investigated at least.

Volcanic eruptions take place here which show subterranean fires. The result is terrible. Millions are destroyed. Millions more are maimed for life. And yet the human family is hardly aware of the **location** of this terrible zone. Would it not be **wiser** and **safer** to teach our children more **mental geography** and less African and Asiatic?

WHY SOME BOYS CANNOT RAISE A MUSTACHE.

Suppose a boy resembles his mother and she resembles her mother, she will be very feminine. He will probably have the upper face of his mother and particularly the upper lip. If he has a very feminine upper lip he will never produce a heavy mustache however much he may shave it and use hair developers. The **masculine** nature is not there and therefore he cannot produce that which must come from masculine faculties.

It is a question of faculty. No woman will have beard unless she has some masculine faculties.

Some of these are Causality, Self-Esteem, Amativeness, Destructiveness, Firmness, and Combativeness.

Any young man who has a strong degree of these six faculties will have little trouble in producing a mustache; in fact it will **produce itself,** or in other words it will have back of it those qualities that build a large upper lip and then adorn it with hair.

LOOK ARIGHT.

Look for sociality and affection in the back head.

Look for pride, will and ambition in the crown of the head.

Look for force, cunning and avarice in the side head.

Look for taste and constructiveness in the upper side temples.

Look for reliability, sympathy and spirituality in the whole top head.

Look for observation and practical talent in the lower forehead.

Look for thought, reason and originality in the upper forehead.

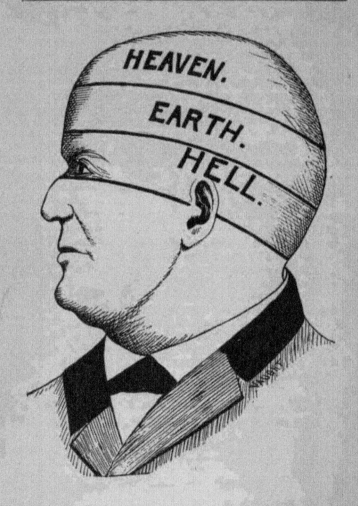

These three divisions of the head represent three divisions of the mind corresponding in nature to the names here.

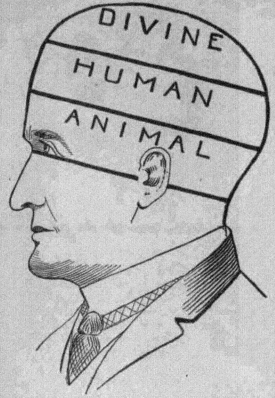

The three-fold nature of human nature is illustrated in the above.

LOVE OF THE OCCULT.

There is a faculty called Spirituality that gives one a love of the mysterious, supernatural and occult. When highly developed and Ideality and Sublimity are also positive, one will have a great attraction toward hypnotism, theosophy, spiritualism, astrology, metaphysics and all kinds of occult thought and manifestations. With these three faculties very weak the opposite will be true.

Cautiousness and the other faculties that unite with it to produce fear.

Fear of Death—Vitativeness and Cautiousness.
Fear of God—Veneration and Cautiousness.
Fear of Ridicule—Approbativeness and Cautiousness.
Pecuniary Fear—Acquisitiveness and Cautiousness.
Parental Fear—Parental Love and Cautiousness.
Superstitious Fear—Spirituality and Cautiousness.
Spontaneous Fear—Cautiousness.

INFIDELITY.

The positive cause of Infidelity is Amativeness. When this faculty is strong and the faculties of Conscientiousness, Benevolence, Friendship and Self-esteem not so strong, infidelity to wife or husband may come about. There can be no certainty in human character without at least a strong faculty of Conscientiousness. For the good of all concerned we affirm that when the elements of Self-esteem and Conscientiousness are weak in any man or woman there will be much likelihood of infidelity.

Oh, men and women, learn to read character element by element!

THE CORN FACULTY

Or the Exact Source of Corns.

Few would believe at first thought that there is a direct relation between a human faculty and corns, but such is a fact. Corns and bunions are nearly all produced by one faculty. It is not exactly a corn faculty. We hardly think corns are of sufficient importance to be honored by Creation with a faculty by which we directly perceive them as the faculty of Color perceives colors. One little corn, if it is properly situated, will come into perfect contact with the whole mind, which is made up of forty-two faculties. No one who has had much experience with corns will doubt the power of a corn to take charge of the larger part of the sensory nervous system and make a sweeping report up to **head**-quarters. Corns do not "just grow." Every product has a proper producer. Corns are produced, not always purposely, but still they are produced. It looks a little strange that one should be endowed with a faculty that will produce corns. We might go further and say that we can tell by an examina-nation of the head, without seeing the walk or taking the trouble to find out whether the shoes are three sizes too small or not, whether one is fertile in the production of corns.

This corn faculty, as we said at the commencement, is not a new faculty. It is as old as the race. It not only produces corns, but many other extraneous, abnormal physical formations. What else could put rings in the lips, deform the skull and produce the **pretty** little feet of the Chinese? It is a contracting faculty. In fact, it is a greater contractor than all the other faculties com-bined. It does not take on contracts, yet it does a large contracting business. It runs many large manufac-tories. It employs hundreds of thousands. It has an af-finity for rich stones, pearls, diamonds, and tombstones. It not only likes the latter while living, but by virtue of its great contracting power often gives those who have not quite such a strong degree of it an untimely chance to place one at the head of the body of one who had it too large.

But a faculty that is strong enough to build a **corset** manufactory can do most anything. It can even tell a "fish story." It is a very lively faculty while it lasts, and its name is not wisdom—but plain Approbativeness.

A poor money saver.

ALTRUISM.

A genuine altruist has Benevolence, Conscientiousness and Friendship predominant.

SOCIALISM.

The socialistic nature is made up of Friendship, Conscientiousness, Benevolence and Ideality, with deficient Self-esteem, Acquisitiveness and Approbativeness. **No one** will be a socialist who has the three last named faculties in the lead.

The above illustration shows that two Roman noses are surely too many in one family, especially in husband and wife.

AFFECTATION.

This unfortunate weakness of human nature comes directly from a single faculty or mental element, to wit: Approbativeness. It is a false desire to please and be agreeable. Conscientiousness and Self-esteem are **always** weak in such people. No one can be affected with these two faculties predominant.

Remember that affectation is always wholly insincere. One can be very bland, affable, deferential, respectful, polite, kind, agreeable and entertaining without an iota of affectation. Just find one with Benevolence, Veneration, Friendship, Suavity, and Conscientiousness strong and you can quickly prove it.

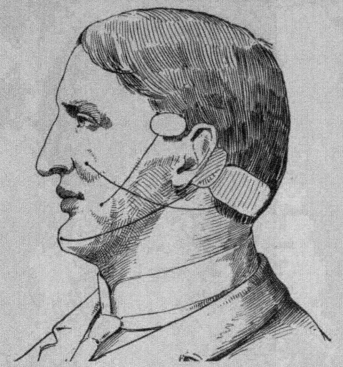

Amativeness, Vitativeness and Alimentiveness with their Heart, Lung and Stomach Centers in the Face.

INTENSITY.

The mental elements that make people intense in their natures are Approbativeness, Destructiveness, Combativeness, Cautiousness, Firmness and Conscientiousness. These faculties key them up to a high pitch. Approbativeness makes one ambitiously intense, Destructiveness forcefully intense, Cautiousness watchfully intense, Combativeness aggressively intense, Conscientiousness dutifully intense and Firmness wilfully intense. Such people lead "strenuous" lives.

The center of human will is defective here.   This illustration shows where Firmness ought to be.

CONSERVATISM.

The mental elements that make conservatism are Cautiousness, Approbativeness, Veneration, Acquisitiveness, Vitativeness and Secretiveness. Find these predominant in the mind and head of anyone and you will find an actual, living, certain conservative.

REV. LYMAN ABBOTT.

A great predominance of the intellectual and moral faculties.

Arthur Flanagan, a child genius.

GENIUS.

Genius is nothing more or less than the inheritance of an unusual degree of one or more faculties. It is a very simple fact.

AMBITION.

Ambition is not energy. It is not industry. Correctly speaking it is a **desire** to be, possess or accomplish some thing. The chief element of it is Approbativeness. This faculty gives all the **desire**. When Self-esteem, Combativeness, Destructiveness and Firmness are added, one will be very energetic in **carrying out** this desire which becomes actual ambition. The distinct kind of ambition will be decided by the other predominant faculty. For instance, if to these five elements is added a predominant element of Acquisitiveness the ambition will be commercial in kind.

DANGEROUSLY   INCOMPETENT.

We pronounce every teacher, parent, minister and reformer who is not thoroughly acquainted with the 42 fundamental faculties of which human beings are composed as **dangerously incompetent**.

This is just as true as it would be for the same parties o practice surgery without a definite knowledge of the arts of the body.

INTELLECTUAL IDIOCY

HUMAN IDIOCY.

One may be idiotic in one thing and at the same time may be a genius along another line. To understand the various kinds of human idiocy one must positively understand the genetic faculties that constitute the human mind.

We give below a fundamental analysis of several distinct kinds of idiocy. For instance, **Social** Idiocy is specifically and fundamentally a very weak degree of the faculties of

> Friendship,
> Conjugality,
> Parental Love,
> Amativeness.

This is absolute truth.

Vital Idiocy is simply and specifically a weak degree of the fundamental faculties of

> Alimentiveness,
> Amativeness,
> Vitativeness.

Moral Idiocy is a weak degree of the fundamental faculties of

> Conscientiousness,
> Benevolence,
> Veneration.

Will Idiocy is a weak degree of the fundamental faculties of

> Firmness,
> Combativeness,
> Destructiveness.

Artistic Idiocy is a weak degree of the fundamental faculties of

> Ideality,
> Sublimity,
> Form,
> Color.

Mechanical Idiocy is a weak degree of the fundamental faculties of

> Constructiveness,
> Size,
> Form.

Mathematical Idiocv is a weak degree of

> Number,
> Causality.

When one has learned the true nature of a single fundamental faculty, he has made the **first** definite step in the understanding of idiocy—or any other condition or power of the human mind.

WHAT MAKES PEOPLE SLOW?

That which makes people slow is a sum of faculties. These are the slow-goers: Cautiousness, Conscientiousness, Causality, Approbativeness, Veneration, Ideality and Order. When anyone has these very much in the lead of all others he will be very cautious, conscientious, thorough, conservative, reverential, painstaking and systematic. Cautiousness puts on the safety brakes, Conscientiousness wants to be sure it is right, Causality wishes to know the reasons for the proposed move, Approbativeness waits for somebody to set the style, Veneration clings to the good old customs, Ideality wishes to put on some more finishing touches and Order says be systematic about it please. Suppose these faculties were all weak in the mental make-up of one; he would be reckless, inconsiderate, thoughtless, indifferent, irreverent, crude, disorderly, and go it pell-mell, hit-or-miss without a semblance of prudent consideration.

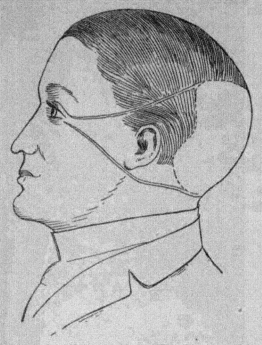

EYES AND HEAD.

Eyes and heads **go together**. Probably very few have thought of this. Eyes are not **merely** organs of vision. More nearly than any other facial features they may express character: in other words, their possibility in the expression of character is more varied and complete. It might be said correctly that they express all phases of character in a **transient** way. They cannot express all the faculties in a **permanent** way very well. What we mean is that the position of the muscles around the eyes will not represent strikingly each individual faculty. But this much is certain, every sentiment is expressed through the eyes. This is not done with the **eyeballs** but with the **lids** that cover the eyeballs. It is almost wholly the **contraction** and **relaxation** of the lids that gives **expression** to the eyes.

A secretive eye, for instance, is secretive because the
lids are put into a secretive position. This particular position is not an open one. Secretiveness **does not
open** the eyes. It **cannot** act upon the eyes in this
way. On the contrary, it gently and yet somewhat
tightly closes them. It **shuts up** the eyes to a great degree. It **draws down the curtains** over the eyeballs.
When one wishes to shut off the public from gazing in
at his windows he pulls down the curtains; when one
wants to shut off strangers from **gazing into his soul** he
shuts down his **soul windows** and pulls down the curtains
until he can see **out only through little slits between the
lids,**

The relation between the eyes and the head, then, is a relation of cause and effect, and is as close as cause and effect; it would be more nearly correct to say that the relation is between faculties and the eyes. Faculties are always mental and simply express themselves first through the head; yet in every normal instance the eyes will correspond with the **formation** of the head. For instance, if one has more brain in his back-head than anywhere else, he will have loving, affectionate eyes; he will have eyes that speak love, and glow with friendship. He will have the eyes of the husband, the wife, the friend, the brother, the sister, the mother, the father, and sometimes all of these mixed.

The eyes, therefore, not only express transient activities of the mind, but if certain faculties of the mind positively predominate in the mental constitution there will be a permanent formation of the eyes. Affectionate eyes are rather thick-lidded, somewhat open, soft, slightly inclined to droop, nicely curved, prominent, larger than small, without any strong angular or straight lines. Love never makes a **straight** line. It is not **hard** enough to make a straight line.

In contrast with these, if heads are very broad from ear to ear or in the middle lobes, and the back-head is only fairly developed, there will be cunning, cautious, hard, revengeful, grasping, coarse eyes. These are made by the faculties in the **side-head**. In other words, they are made by Combativeness, Destructiveness, Vitativeness, Secretiveness, Cautiousness, Acquisitiveness and Alimentiveness. If these faculties **positively** predominate in one's mental make-up, the eyes will be a striking contrast to the eyes just mentioned. When one sees eyes that are closely shut, the upper lid coming hard down upon the ball, and they look sideways and out of the corners frequently, he may put it down that such eyes represent selfish, dangerous and unreliable people.

The dark area covers all of the head territory of selfishness that can be seen from a side view.   Do not look anywhere else for it upon the head.

HUMAN NATURE OF TRUSTS.

The fundamental elements of human nature that give a love of trusts are Acquisitiveness, Approbativeness, Self-esteem, Firmness, Combativeness and Destructiveness.   It is specifically a love of financial power and these selfish elements, with Acquisitiveness in the lead, constitute just this kind of human nature.

As is the head so is the body. The outline of one head here is almost wholly mental and the body is very frail and delicate correspondingly. The outline of the other is positively vital, and you can see the difference in physical development.

MODESTY.

Genuine modesty is the product of Ideality, Conscientiousness, Veneration and Approbativeness with weak faculties of Self-esteem, Amativeness and Alimentiveness.

AGREEABLENESS.

The agreeable elements of human nature are Friendship, Benevolence, Veneration, Suavity, Approbativeness and Conscientiousness. Each of these in its own way tries to be agreeable, and when all are strong one is friendly, gentle, respectful, affable, catering and accommodating.

BEAUTY.

To be beautiful in face and body is to be endowed with a predominating degree of Ideality, Parental Love, Amativeness, Conjugality, Alimentiveness, Human Nature, Suavity, Benevolence, Conscientiousness, Hope, Spirituality, Comparison, Mirthfulness, and Causality. These faculties give health, magnetism, a fine physical figure, shapely hands, a well formed neck, red and nicely curved lips, a fine nose and beautiful, sincere, lustrous, intelligent eyes.

If Alimentiveness is too large, one will be too fat; if Destructiveness, Combativeness and Firmness are predominant, too angular and bony; if Approbativeness, is in the lead, too vain and affected; if Hope and Mirthfulness are too weak, one will be "long-faced," and if Amativeness is too weak one will have a poor physical form.

If one would be beautiful let her keep in good health Amativeness and Alimentiveness and cultivate Ideality, Mirthfulness, Hope, Conscientiousness, Causality, Comparison, Friendship, Benevolence, Parental Love, Conjugality and Spirituality.

FORCEFUL RESISTANCE.

Forceful resistance in children, women and men comes directly from Combativeness, Destructiveness and Firmness. Any man woman, or child who has a strong degree of these three faculties will be very forceful in resistance in either a mental or physical way. If to these three faculties are added strong faculties of Approbativeness and Self-esteem, there will be a whirlwind of forceful, determined resistance.

INTUITION.

The faculty called Human Nature is the center of intuition. The talent for character reading and diagnosing diseases comes principally from this faculty. The nature, disposition or character of anything or anyone is known instinctively by this element of mind. Strictly speaking, it is the only intuitional faculty. Other faculties like Spirituality and Benevolence aid it, by giving a general psychical and tender nature, but these have no intuition in and of themselves.

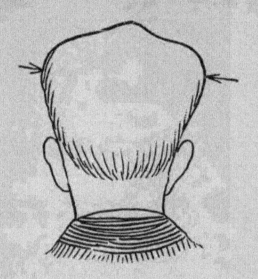

Here is cautiousness extremely developed from a back view. Such people hesitate and manifest timidity and even cowardice.

PROCRASTINATION.

A procrastinator is strongly endowed with Cautiousness and negatively endowed with Combativeness, Self-esteem, Destructiveness, Firmness, Approbativeness and Conscientiousness. General McClellan of the Civil war was constituted somewhat this way. Anyone strongly equipped with the six last-named faculties will be ready in decision, quick in action and take right hold of what he is to do and do it up with dispatch. He likes to do a thing then and there. He has the courage and force to carry out his judgment and sense of duty.

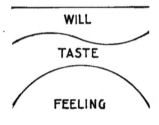

WILL.

Will makes straight lines and angles. If these predominate in the face and head, Will will predominate in the mind.

TASTE.

Taste runs to curves. The more curved lines in the face and head the more artisitc taste in the mind.

FEELING.

Feelings tend toward roundness. When roundness predominates in head and face feeling predominates in the mind.

SUSCEPTIBILITY TO INSANITY.

The mind elements that give one susceptibility to insanity are Spirituality, Cautiousness, Veneration, Approbativeness, Conscientiousness, Parental Love, Friendship, Conjugality, Ideality and Constructiveness. These give keen susceptibility to hallucinations, delusions, fears, remorses, criticisms, failures, blues, griefs, disappointments and false imaginations.

Spirituality is the center of susceptibility to delusions, hallucinations and in connection with Veneration, of religious insanity.

Cautiousness is the center of fears of danger and in union with Approbativeness of despondency and melancholia.

Constructiveness is the center of invention and when too strong in one he is liable to have "wheels in his head."

Spirituality, Veneration, Cautiousness and Approbativeness have caused the largest number of insane cases.

There is a mild form of insanity very prevalent in this country now, caused by the faculties of Ideality and Spirituality.

The inherent preventitives of Insanity are the faculties of Human Nature, Causality, Self-esteem, Combativeness, Firmness, Hope and Mirthfulness. If these are weak, one is liable to go to that excess that some mental derangement will occur.

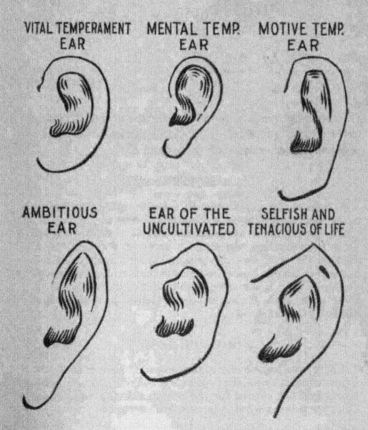

VITAL TEMPERAMENT EAR   MENTAL TEMP. EAR   MOTIVE TEMP. EAR

AMBITIOUS EAR   EAR OF THE UNCULTIVATED   SELFISH AND TENACIOUS OF LIFE

Jealousy projects a muscle under the red part of the lower lip, as indicated in the illustration. Notice the jealous, furtive glance of the eye also.

GOSSIPING.

A love of gossip comes directly from Approbativeness, Secretiveness and Destructiveness. Look directly for these three faculties and if they are found in a predominating degree in anyone you may rest assured he or she will gossip. Approbativeness is the captain and its two aids are Secretiveness and Destructiveness. Why? Because Approbativeness likes to excel in something and the other two gladly help it in this kind of distinction.

HOMESICKNESS.

The mental elements that cause "homesickness" are Friendship, Conjugality, Parental Love and Inhabitiveness. It is regard for the inmates of the house that chiefly produces what is termed homesickness.

Alimentiveness or appetite and its connection with the lips.

Two heads and two outlines of face. As is the head, so is the face.

HUNTING.

The **love** of hunting comes from Destructiveness, Combativeness, Secretiveness, Alimentiveness with Approbativeness. The **skill** from Human Nature, Secretiveness, Individuality, Locality, Size, Weight and Amativeness. Human Nature learns the habits of game. Secretiveness gives the foxy desire to catch. Individuality the ability to spot single objects. Size, to measure distance in shooting. Weight, the intuitive perception of where to shoot. Locality the love and ability to travel, and Amativeness the power to co-ordinate or use the muscles all together.

UNSTEADINESS.

The matter with people who are unsteady is a deficiency of the faculties of Firmness, Self-esteem, Continuity and Conscientiousness. These round out the crown of the head. If the crown of anyone's head is flat or deficient in development it may be put down as a certainty that the party will be fickle, restless, unstable, and generally unreliable in fulfilling promises and sticking to undertakings. These are the elements of mind that give steadiness and stability and this part of the head you must look to for such a character.

POINTERS.

The broader the head the more selfishness.
The higher the crown the more pride.
The fuller the backhead the more affection.
The fuller the upper side temples the more taste.
The fuller the lower forehead the more practicality.
The fuller the upper forehead and the less the lower the more theory.
The rounder the head the more feeling.
The more square the head the more thought and exactness.
The less basilar development the less animal.
The narrower the head the less force.
The less backhead the colder the disposition.
The more closed the eyes the more secrecy.
The higher the eyebrows from the pupils of the eyes the more credulity.
The more middle face the more energy.
The more lower face the more sensuality.
The finer the hair the finer the brain.
The tougher the hair the tougher the brain.
The thicker the scalp and skull the less brain.
The fuller the whole tophead the more reliability.
The thinner the lips the less affection.
The more the teeth are shown the more love of applause.
The more features that turn upward the more cheerfulness.
The more affectation in the voice the less substantial character.
The more boastfulness the less courage.

TEASING.

The desire to tease comes from Destructiveness, Mirthfulness, Combativeness and Approbativeness. Destructiveness is rough and likes to get others into trouble. Mirthfulness enjoys all the fun there is in it. Combativeness gives the love of conflict and Approbativeness crows over the success. These are the teasers, sure.

D. L. Moody represents in his head formation a great deal of human energy.

THE TWO POSITIVELY ENERGETIC DIVISIONS OF THE MIND.

The two positively energetic divisions of the mind are found in the sidehead and crown. Anyone with both of these divisions highly developed will be positively energetic.   Then look for a broad head and high crown for positive energy.

AN OUTLINE OF A FUNDAMENTAL SYSTEM OF CHARACTER READING.

First. INHERITED faculties.

Second. NATIVE difference in the size of these faculties.

Third.   The LOCALIZATION of these faculties.

Fourth.   THEIR brain organs.

Fifth.   The SIZE of these brain organs.

Sixth.   The SHAPE of the head that the unequal size of these organs causes.

Seventh.   The SIZE OF THE HEAD that is the RESULT of the SIZE of the FORTY-TWO FACULTIES.

Eighth.   The QUALITY of the WHOLE body that is GROWN by these faculties.   If certain faculties PREDOM-

INATE, the body must NECESSARILY be of a certain quality.

Ninth.   The TEMPERAMENT that is the RESULT of a PREDOMINANCE of certain faculties.

Tenth.   The INDIVIDUAL anatomy that is the NECESSARY RESULT OF A PREDOMINATING temperament.

Eleventh.   The physiognomy that is a NECESSARY CONSEQUENCE of faculties expressing themselves by means of the facial anatomy and physiology.

Twelfth.   The general physiology of the body that is the necessary CONCOMITANT of the forty-two faculties.

PATIENCE.

What is the stuff out of which patience is made? The warp and woof of patience is Conscientiousness, Cautiousness, Ideality, Order, Causality, Benevolence, Veneration, Spirituality, Firmness, Continuity, Conjugality, Parental Love, Hope and Friendship. The four chief elements of patience are Conscientiousness, Ideality, Continuity and Firmness. Anyone with these four faculties very strong will be patient.

Conscientiousness likes conscientious labor; Ideality likes to finish off; Continuity likes to continue along the line started upon, and Firmness likes to persevere. When Approbativeness, Self-esteem, Destructiveness, Combativeness, Alimentiveness and Acquisitiveness are dominant in adults or children, impatience will be manifested frequently.

WHO ARE SUSPICIOUS?

The suspicious have Secretiveness, Approbativeness, Acquisitiveness, Amativeness and Cautiousness highly developed. These selfish elements predominant would make an angel suspicious. Such people are naturally cunning, deceitful, selfish, jealous and fearful, and spontaneously produce ideas that nearly everybody else are. They take their own minds as standards and instinctively believe that "All are rogues till proven innocent." There is no other way to be suspicious. You can always find some of these faculties strong in suspicious people and Conscientiousness, Benevolence and Spirituality weak.

FRANCIS REA McMILLEN

A Musical Genius.

HENRY GEORGE.

Fine forehead with a great development of the frontal part of the tophead showing a very positive degree of Benevolence.

A TRINITY OF TRAITORS.

Human Treachery is a fact. Fortunately, it is not a very common fact; yet it has occurred. Probably all of our readers have had a little taste of it. Three of the forty-two elements of which human nature is composed may be called treacherous. Either of these three will go back on acquaintance, friend or kindred. When they are fully understood, one understands the very foundation of treachery. They are Amativeness, Acquisitiveness and Approbativeness. Either one may be treacherous when in the lead. Amativeness has proved treacherous thousands of times in love. Those who have this faculty positively predominant are very treacherous, so far as constancy and reliability are concerned in association, love and marriage. The flirt, the sensualist, the bigamist and the seducer are living examples. In itself this faculty has no regard for the welfare of the one in which it is interested for the moment. Only when it unites with some of the higher faculties can it be helpful. Therefore all who depend upon this kind of love or this faculty in association, companionship, courtship, prospective marriage and marriage itself will be positively disappointed. It is not reliable unless sustained by higher faculties like Conjugality, Friendship and Conscientiousness.

Again, Acquisitiveness is treacherous. How little it takes sometimes, of money, to prove unreliable. How many will sell their souls for a "mess of pottage." Some can even be bought for a dollar. Acquisitiveness itself is positively selfish. It looks out for No. 1 wholly. If money is the root of all evil, this faculty is the root of all evil. It is the only faculty that loves money. When sufficiently strong it will go back on friends, kindred and country. It will prove traitor to every obligation and all kinds of domestic and civic responsibility.

Again, Approbativeness is treacherous. It is the center of ambition. To attain fame and excel somebody for the sake of the plaudits of the world, this faculty makes thousands treacherous. Some politicians are treacherous. This is the center of selfish politics. If this faculty positively dominates there is no certainty of honesty and reliability. It makes many untruthful. It causes them to use all kinds of deceit. It is altogether the most deceitful faculty of the forty-two. It is the most pretentious. It is the center of affectation, false modesty, false pretenses and false everything.

These three faculties can be spotted. The traitors of human nature can be distinctly known and distinctly located. The other thirty-nine together have probably never done 1-100th as much treacherous work as these three have. Nearly all human treachery can be traced to one or more of these three faculties.

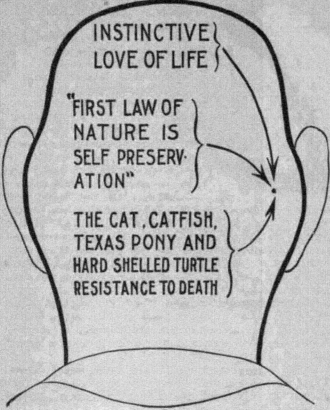

INSTINCTIVE
LOVE OF LIFE

"FIRST LAW OF
NATURE IS
SELF PRESERV-
ATION"

THE CAT, CATFISH,
TEXAS PONY AND
HARD SHELLED TURTLE
RESISTANCE TO DEATH

Use your own eyes and notice how enormously developed people are right behind the ears who are very tenacious of life. One can see such development at a glance, ten to twenty feet away.

VITALITY.

Vitality is specifically inherent in Alimentiveness. Secondarily in Amativeness. To these add the element of Vitativeness and you have innate love of life, as well as vitality. Together they give all there is of vitality and constitute what is called constitution.

HOW TO READ THE NOSE.

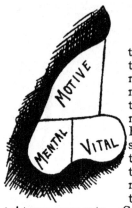

The nose may be divided into three distinct parts as indicated in the above figure. The bony part represents the Motive Temperament. The tip represents the Mental Temperament. The wings represent the Vital Temperament. How true this is may be clearly seen in very marked cases of each temperament. Take a distinct Vital Temperament and study the nose that goes with it and then do the same with the Motive and Mental temperaments. Generals Sheridan, Sherman, Logan, Miles, Napoleon, Moltke, Napier had or have Motive noses. So has Admiral Dewey. So had Lincoln and Grant. Washington and Beecher had the three more nearly equal. Lord Salisbury, Robert Ingersoll, Senator Mason and Dwight L. Moody show plenty of the vital part of the nose.

Herbert Spencer, Eugene Field and Robert Louis Stevenson show a distinct predominance of the Mental part. It is a question of the **predominance** of faculties. A distinct Vital Temperament cannot produce a Mental form of nose.

Noses mean something. They have **direct causes.** These are the faculties. They may be much **mixed, but** in such cases the faculties and temperaments will be correspondingly mixed.

As is the **head** so is the **temperament** and as is the temperament so is the **nose**.

PEOPLE WHOM ANIMALS LOVE.

Some people attract animals. Why? Because they have strong Friendship, Parental Love and Amativeness. Any man, woman or child with these **three** faculties very strong will attract animals. No one **with an** undeveloped backhead will attract and pet **animals.**

FANATICISM

You can prove the truthfulness of the above by using your own eyes and minds.

FANATICISM.

A fanatic is one with Veneration, Spirituality, Conscientiousness and Approbativeness positively strong and especially Veneration. There is no other way under the sun for one to be a fanatic.

HANDIWORK.

To do handiwork successfully is to possess a good degree of the following elements: Individuality, Size, Form, Weight, Locality, Color, Order, Number and Constructiveness These are the faculties that the eyes and hands require to see objects quickly and accurately and to measure, weigh, touch, color, arrange, number and place them.

A SIGN OF IGNORANCE.

All who facetiously or otherwise use the word "bump" when speaking of the forty-two or more primary faculties that constitute human nature and use localized brain centers, expose their own ignorance. There is a world of difference between **formation** and "bump."

ABSENT-MINDEDNESS.

With weak faculties of Secretiveness, Cautiousness, Approbativeness, Human Nature and Individuality and strong faculties of Causality, Ideality, Sublimity, Spirituality and Conscientiousness one will be amusingly and humiliatingly absent-minded.

SUPERSTITION.

Superstition has a perfectly definite source—the faculty of Spirituality. No one can be at all superstitious without this faculty. It is the only faculty that gives anyone any sense of and confidence in the mystic. To be superstitious, then, is to have a positive development of this faculty. The particular kind of superstition will be decided by the other strongest faculty in one's mental make-up.

If Cautiousness and Vitativeness unite with Spirituality one will expect death; if Parental love and Cautiousness are strong, he will expect the death of a child. Always remember that Spirituality is that element of mind that gives one confidence in number thirteen, Friday, a new moon or a jackrabbit's foot as a good or bad sign, omen or mascot.

A superstitious fear of the Devil is caused by Spirituality, Cautiousness, Conscientiousness, Veneration, Destructiveness and Secretiveness. A superstitious fear of God is the product of Spirituality, Veneration, Cautiousness, Vitativeness and Conscientiousness. When Human Nature and Causality are predominant and Spirituality and Veneration negative one will be inclined to pooh-pooh all so-called signs and omens.

A STANDARD
OF
LAZINESS

We want all our readers to fix this head and face in their minds. It is a positive standard of constitutional laziness.

LAZINESS.

Genuine laziness is the result of deficient Destructiveness, Combativeness, Approbativeness, Acquisitiveness, Self-esteem, Firmness and Conscientiousness. No one really likes hard work of any kind who is weak in the faculties of Destructiveness and Combativeness. These two faculties are the fundamental causes of positive energy of some kind. Just what they will like to do is determined by some other strong faculty. If Acquisitiveness is strong they will work for money or property. If Approbativeness is strong, for fame and victory.

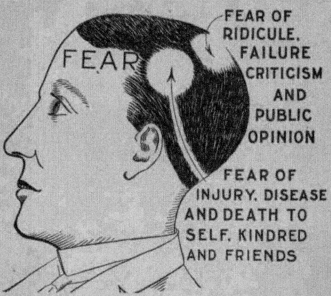

FEAR

FEAR OF RIDICULE, FAILURE CRITICISM AND PUBLIC OPINION

FEAR OF INJURY, DISEASE AND DEATH TO SELF, KINDRED AND FRIENDS

Here is a whole volume of truth in a few words. Anyone can overwhelmingly demonstrate the truthfulness of this by careful observation and examination.

FEAR.

There are two elements of fear in the human mind— fear of danger and fear of criticism. These come from Cautiousness and Approbativeness respectively. This absolute truth. No other part of the mind can feel fear whatever. Go directly then to these two faculties for fear. What one will fear about most is determined by the other larger faculties.

BORROWING TROUBLE.

There are only two trouble borrowing elements in human nature. All who borrow trouble must do so by means of one or both of these. All apprehension, expectation and anticipation of a **troublesome** kind is produced by the elemental faculties of Cautiousness and Approbativeness. To understand why one borrows trouble is to understand the nature of these two mental elements. To tell in advance whether one will borrow trouble is to decide how large these two faculties are in one's make-up. They can be depended upon to borrow trouble just as certainly as they are large enough and especially when they predominate over all others. Then they will borrow worlds of trouble. Other faculites may **trouble** one but they never **borrow** trouble.

HESITATION.

A hesitator is strongly endowed with Cautiousness, Approbativeness and Conscientiousness. These give one respectively, fear of danger, fear of ridicule and fear of doing wrong, and therefore hesitation.

BASHFULNESS.

Bashfulness almost wholly comes from the faculty of Approbativeness. If to this faculty is added large faculties of Cautiousness, Veneration, Ideality and Conscientiousness, there will be a complete bashful tendency. Then if Self-esteem and Combativeness are weak one will be **positively** bashful.

COWARDICE.

Cowardice emanates from the faculty of Cautiousness chiefly. This faculty with Vitativeness causes physical cowardice. Moral cowardice chiefly comes from Approbativeness. This faculty or element of human nature makes one afraid of public opinion. The genuine, all around coward, therefore, is weak in Conscientiousness, Self-esteem, Combativeness, Friendship, Conjugality, Parental Love, and Benevolence, and strong in Cautiousness, Approbativeness and Vitativeness.

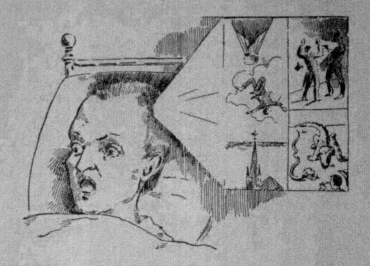

The above illustration is full of meaning. Many have frightful dreams. They spring from a very active condition of Cautiousness. One gets into all kinds of dangers while asleep when this faculty is very large.

REASON.

To reason is to have Causality and Comparison. No other faculties can think in any way or degree. This is a very important fact.

MARVELOUS.

The most marvelous fact in all history and in human life today is the extreme ignorance of the majority of the world's teachers concerning the constitution of human nature. Statesmen, jurists and presidents of universities are marvelously ignorant of the elements that constitute this constitution.

A STRIKING ILLUSTRATION OF THE MARVEL-
OUS ABSURDITY OF HAVING A VITAL FACE
AND BODY ON A MENTAL HEAD.

Heads do not grow on bodies. The absolutely opposite
is true. The head is **headquarters** for all else below.

Faculties have their headquarters in the brain. They
build the brain for their uses. That is what is is for.
By means of the brain they build the body and run it.
Study the illustration. Observe the non-correspondence
between head and face. Did you ever see that kind of a
face on that kind of a head?

In a **mental** head the base of the brain is relatively
small. When this is so it is an impossibility to possess a
large vital and muscular body, because the vital faculties
have their centers in the base of the brain and this must
be largely developed before there can be a large vital
face and body. As is the mind so is the brain and as is
the brain so is the face.

WHERE THE PRESIDENTIAL BEE BUZZES.

The buzzing of the presidential bee is nowhere else than in the faculty of Approbativeness.   No further explanation is needed.

COURAGE.

There are two kinds of courage.   Hence there are two centers of courage.   Combativeness is the center of physical courage, Self-esteem of mental courage.

The two together constitute the inherent nature of rage.

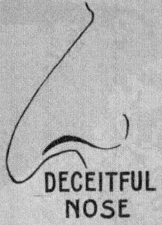

DECEITFUL NOSE

Remember this nose when you deal with people.

GAMBLING.

The very center of the disposition to gamble is combativeness. The second element is Spirituality. The third Secretiveness. The fourth Acquisitiveness.

HOW TO READ CHARACTER FROM GESTURES.

All downward gestures mean a strong faculty of Destructiveness. All flowing or curved gestures mean strong faculties of Time, Weight and Ideality.

All **pointed** gestures mean strong Perceptive faculties with Combativeness, Destructiveness, Conscientiousness and Self-esteem back of them.

All **expansive** gestures mean strong faculties of Sublimity, Ideality, Spirituality and Hope.

All **descriptive** gestures of objects mean strong Perceptive faculties.

All gestures mean force, feeling, imagination and perceptive intellect stronger than Causality, Firmness and Self-esteem. These three last named faculties give a cool, dignified, self-controlled, logical cast of mind that enables one to reason in a very calm, judicial way without giving way to force, feeling and gesture.

MIXED HEADS AND FACES.

A human being is composed of masculine and feminine faculties. Not equally, however. One may inherit the feminine faculties decidedly in the lead of the masculine. Another may inherit the forty-two faculties in a reversed condition. Sometimes a whole group of feminine faculties are inherited. When this is the case then a corresponding whole degree of that part of the brain that these faculties use is built up in feminine form and also the face. This is mixed inheritance. It results in mixed heads, faces and bodies.

Study the two illustrations. The first is the opposite of the second. In it all above the line is feminine; nose, eyes, brows, forehead and tophead. Here you see the true feminine form of head and face as far as it extends. All below the line is masculine; neck, jaws, chin, mouth, backhead and back tophead.

Certain faculties are fundamentally and always masculine. The only way to understand masculinity is to understand the **faculties** of masculinity. No one can have a masculine nature, head, face, body and voice, without a predominance of certain faculties that are masculine. This is just as true of feminine nature, head, face, body and voice. Masculine faculties are more positive in their nature and form head, face and body in angular lines. Feminine faculties are more negative in their nature and form head, face and body in curved lines.

HUMAN ATTRACTION.

Two **opposite** divisions of human nature are struggling for the mastery. It is a contest between the faculties of the frontal brain and the faculties of the occipital brain—between the **intellectual** faculties and the **social faculties**—between the school-room and the home, the studio and the club-room, books and balls, thought and sentiment, study and society, learning and entertainment—"hard application" and a "good time." Parents realize the actual reality of it; so do teachers. It is a serious problem for many.

The social faculties are five in number. They are all grouped together in the backhead, or, more properly, the cerebellum and the occipital lobes of the cerebrum. Externally they cover about the head territory indicated in the illustration. Their names are Amativeness, Conjugality, Parental Love, Inhabitiveness and Friendship. These five faculties like home, association, courtship, marriage, domestic life, the fireside, parties, entertainments, weddings, picnics, clubs, balls and "gay times." They are directly the opposite of the intellectual. As a magnet they come in direct conflict with **intellectual concentration**. They divert the mind from study. The heart of the question of co-education is right here.

The chief intellectual faculties are Causality, Comparison, Eventuality, Number, Language, Human Nature, Constructiveness and Ideality. These give a fundamental love of knowledge for its own sake. They love history, literature, science and philosophy. When these faculties are predominant in a child there will be an instinctive tendency to **books**. Such a child will get knowledge under the most **unfavorable circumstances**.

When both the social and intellectual faculties are strong, and **equally** strong, then comes the "tug of war." Then it is a conflict between the **social magnet** and the **intellectual magnet**.

GULLIBILITY.

Some people are gullible. They are gullible because they have some or all of the following faculties predominant: Spirituality, Conscientiousness, Benevolence, Friendship, Conjugality, Parental Love, Ideality, Sublimity, Approbativeness and the faculties of Human Nature and Secretiveness weak.

Anyone with weak faculties of Secretiveness and Human Nature is open to gullibility. Either of the first named faculties are open doors for confidence men and women. Thousands are fleeced daily, to a greater or less degree, through the faculty of Spirituality. Of all the faculties of the human mind this is the most gullible.

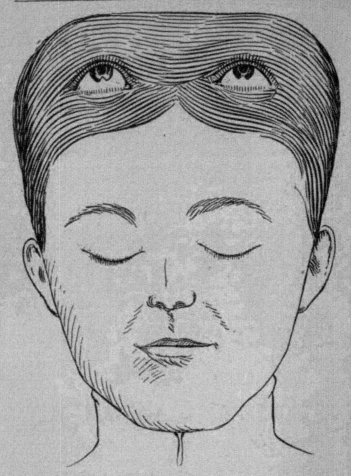

WHAT WE SEE GHOSTS WITH.

Our Spiritual Eyes.

Is there such a thing as spiritual vision?   If there is it is to be found in the function of the faculty of Spirituality. This faculty has been definitely located. The two centers in the brain used by this faculty are located where you see the two eyes. These, therefore, may very properly be called our spiritual eyes. At any rate those who have a strong faculty of Spirituality are more susceptible to all kinds of thoughts of a mystic or psychical kind. They tend instinctively to the occult of some kind—Spiritualism, Theosophy or Astrology. They believe in influences, omens, impressions, spirits and ghosts.

ALL THE SIGNS OF SELFISHNESS.

A closely shut, thick-lidded eye, with the upper lid pressing down so that it makes nearly a horizontal line. When there is also a furtive glance sidewise and a droop at the corner, selfishness is certain.

A thick nose, particularly just above its wings, with a tendency to turn down.

A closely shut mouth, yet thick lips, which do not show the red part very much.

A projection of the muscle under the lower lip causing it to look sullen and jealous.

A large, thick chin, especially one that is thick downward from the corners of the mouth.

A heavy, coarse lower jaw.

A large neck.

Ears in which the lower half is much the stronger.

A voice that is hard and cunning.

A disposition to boast, and particularly to command and domineer.

To be absolutely sure, closely notice the shape of the head. If it is very broad from ear to ear, full all around at the base, very high in the crown and pinched and undeveloped in the upper back head and top head, positive selfishness is an absolute certainty.

Benevolence large with its forehead wrinkles.

HUMAN GOODNESS.

The tophead is the seat of the larger number of the faculties of human goodness. No one **can** be positively reliable without a strong development of Benevolence, Hope, Veneration, Spirituality and Conscientiousness. These fill out, or more correctly round out the tophead. It is not enough for the head to arch beautifully when looked at from a side view. When looked at from a front or back view it may be conical in shape. If so, the faculties of Conscientiousness, Hope and Spirituality will be comparatively weak; hence people with such heads will not be perfectly reliable.

In the center of the frontal half of the tophead is located the faculty of Benevolence. The illustration shows the location and a strong degree of the faculty.

Be very careful to locate it correctly, and then judge of its development by ascertaining if the head is convex, plane or concave at this location. In a few cases it may be found so much stronger than the surrounding faculties that it will stand out alone very much like the half of a sphere. It affects a frontal muscle that covers the forehead until it makes little horizontal wrinkles across the forehead, as may be seen in the illustration.

It may properly be called the kindly feeling. It is the opposite of Destructiveness. It is the most tender element of the human soul. It counteracts human selfishness. It is one of the human civilizers. It is the chief element of generosity, charity and humanitarianism. If this section of the head is low and flat there will be little kindness manifested and practically no humanitarianism. It is the opposite of hatred, revenge and ferocity. Faith, hope and charity, but the greatest of these is charity

The reason the lips meet in the kiss is because the affectionate faculties have their nervous centers in the lips.

HOW CHARACTER OUTS.

Allan Pinkerton, the great detective, took for his **rule** "murder will out." This is just as true of human character. In fact it **stands exposed** all of the time. It is exactly like a language. He who understands a language can read it anywhere and at all times. The human body **completely exposes** one all of the time. Why? Because it **wholly represents** and **indicates** all of the human nature or mind that uses it. "He that has eyes to see let him see."

Faculties have a **sixfold way** of expressing or exposing themselves.

Phrenologically through their brain organs.

Physiognomically through their facial centers.

Temperamentally through brain and body.

Qualitatively in organic quality.

Motionally through all movements.

Vocally through the voice.

Take the faculty of Combativeness for illustration. This faculty expresses itself in a positive development of the head about one inch and a half back from the center of the tip of each ear.

It exposes itself in a convex form of the lower half of the nose.

It exposes itself in a compact, wiry quality of the body.

It exposes itself in the motive temperament.

It exposes itself in a high-pitched, courageous, contentious voice.

It exposes itself in throwing the head a little backward and to one side, in a springy walk and defensive attitude of the body.

In this sixfold way nearly all faculties expose themselves.

So that he who runs may read, if he will but learn and feel, and look and listen.

This is scientific, systematic, character reading.

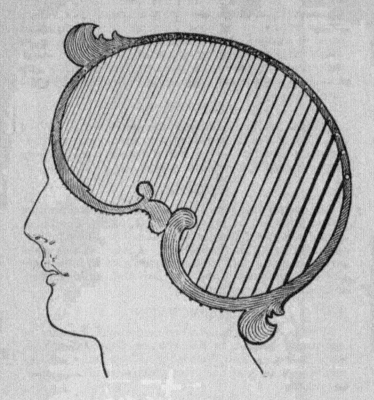

A HARP OF FORTY-TWO STRINGS.

A human being is a harp of forty-two totally different strings. All of the music and discord of human association is performed on these strings. They are **elemental** strings. They never wear out. If played upon properly, they grow stronger instead of weaker. In this they are unlike the strings of all other musical instruments. Their power is in action. These strings can be developed. They are not in an equal degree of strength

at birth.   If they were, all would naturally be in tune.
The majority of the human family are out of tune.   These
strings are not in harmony; they do not in many cases
work in unison.   They constitute, however, the most
wonderful instrument in existence.   We should know
them more fully even than we know the strings of any
man-made instrument.   We should know how to handle
them properly.

RETICENCE.

Instinctive reticence springs from Secretiveness.   When
it is dominant in the mental organization of one and Cautiousness, Human Nature and Firmness are also very
strong one will be a veritable sphinx.

CURIOSITY.

The mental elements that constitute the composition
of curiosity are Secretiveness, Spirituality, Sublimity,
Approbativeness, Amativeness, Ideality, Individuality,
Causality and Constructiveness.   These faculties when
strong enough in one's make-up will give an intense desire to see or know things that are new, novel, hidden,
mystical, strange and unusual.

ACCOMMODATING.

Why is one naturally accommodating?   Because he
has strong elements of Benevolence, Conscientiousness,
Approbativeness and Friendship.   These four mind elements together give one great pleasure in accommodating others.

BOASTFULNESS.

To boast is to have a strong faculty of Approbativeness.   No other element cares to boast.   Then, if Conscientiousness is rather weak and Self-esteem and Combativeness fairly strong one will be addicted to great
boastfulness.

NEATNESS.

The innate elements of neatness are Ideality, Sublimity and Order.   Add to these Approbativeness and Self-
esteem to give the **pride** to be neat, and you have **actual
neatness.**

WHY SANTA COMES AND HOW HE GETS HERE.

Even an imaginary character can be fully interpreted by means of predominant faculties. Such a jolly, cunning, child-loving old soul as Santa Claus could only exist in fact or fiction by possessing a great degree of the following faculties:

1. Benevolence.
2. Comparison.
3. Mirthfulness.
4. Constructiveness.
5. Locality.
6. Weight.

7. Cautiousness.
8. Secretiveness.
9. Destructiveness.
10. Friendship.
11. Parental Love.

Parental Love and Friendship wake him up from his long, long slumber. Destructiveness enables him to "get a move on himself." He goes about slyly and cautiously at **night** by means of Secretiveness and Cautiousness. He finds his way by means of Locality, and noiselessly climbs to the tops of houses and down the chimneys by means of Weight.

He is very ingenious and a great judge of **mechanical** toys, because of his large Constructiveness.

Look at the merry, cunning twinkle in his eye. This comes from Mirthfulness in conjunction with Secretiveness. He also has sharp classifying power. He grades his goods nicely. He recognizes the eternal fitness of things. He does the right thing at the right time. Comparison enables him to do this. He not only loves children, but is a natural humanitarian. He is a kindly old fellow. Good nature beams from his physiognomy. He seems to be at peace with the whole world. This broad, general, helpful disposition springs from a large faculty of Benevolence. These are his predominating faculties. They are quite accurately localized by the figures 1 to 11 in the two outlines of his head.

His face is also an interesting study. Notice the round convex formation of his cheeks. This indicates wonderful lung power. His circulation must be excellent. This enables him to stand the coldest climate. All in all, he is a merry old fellow.

WILL.

The two principal elements of the human will are Firmness and Combativeness. Take these two elements and add any other and you will have any particular kind of will. These and Conscientiousness make a moral will. These and Destructiveness, a forceful will. These and Approbativeness, an ambitional will. These and Acquisitiveness constitute a commercial will.

LOOK ON THIS AND THEN ON THAT.

WHAT TWO PICTURES TELL.

Study these two pictures. They tell a graphic story. And yet heads mean nothing—to some people. Why not be candid? Where is the wisdom of being blind—of having eyes and seeing not?

What's the use of being prejudiced?

The above is the outline of a head in which the thinking, moral and esthetic faculties are dominant. In fact, all of the higher faculties are dominant. This is shown by the high forehead, the broad temples, the high frontal tophead and the expansion of the upper half of the backhead. These are the seats of all the better, cheerful, unselfish, humane, refined, esthetic, moral and spiritual faculties. When predominant they shape the head as shown. As is the head so will be the face. Observe the face. How cheerful, refined, generous, friendly, tender, true and happy.

Compare it with this. Observe that the shape of the head here is the very opposite of the other. See how the face corresponds. One is the **antithesis** of the other. And yet there is nothing in heads and faces; nothing in Phrenology and Physiognomy! Let us see if there is not. Which of these two would you rather **meet on a lonely highway?** Ah, ha! You would rather meet the first, would you? We thought so. When it comes to a practical test; a real, selfish dollars and cents, life or death situation, then all drop their prejudices and accept Phrenology and Physiognomy in a hurry.

CHARACTER IN ACTION.

To get at character definitely one must understand clearly the fundamental elements of character. For instance, Destructiveness is a fundamental element. The word does not indicate its true nature, however. The function of the faculty is more nearly **force** than anything else. It is the only faculty that likes to **move** without an object in view. In other words, it likes motion for its own sake. To move, walk, play, run, jump, strike, hammer and kick is its pleasure. It will cause a child to do all of this without any object in view. It is a reservoir of positive force. When very strong it must have action. This action is always more or less rough. Everything one touches who has this faculty very strong **feels** it. It is the opposite of tenderness. It charges the whole body with positive force. It takes hold of any article with a strong grip. It will almost crush your hand in the handshake.

It likes to tie a **tight** knot. In a business man it likes solid, heavy goods, instead of laces, batting and feathers. In its lower combinations it will enjoy blasting rock. It is the principal faculty in "clatter" and "racket." Three or four children with it large can indeed make a fearful racket. It delights in loud noises. The one day in the year that it likes better than all others is July the 4th. It likes the whirr of the planing-mill. It likes to go at a thing "hammer and tongs." A child with this faculty large will not cry as easily as one with it small. It is one of the elements of grit. It likes nothing tame. It is the only faculty that thunders in the voice. It growls in the bull-dog. It roars in the lion. All profanity that does not come from this faculty is counterfeit. No Destructiveness, no malice.

It adds the quality of force to every mental or physical effort. It may be entirely too strong for the restraining faculties of Benevolence, Conscientiousness, Approbativeness, Cautiousness and the Affections to govern. When this is so then it is dangerous.

Acquisitiveness in head and face or the money-lover.

INCREDULITY.

The incredulous are weak in the faculties of Spirituality, Conscientiousness, Veneration, Ideality and Sublimity and strong in the faculties of Human Nature, Comparison, Causality and Secretiveness.

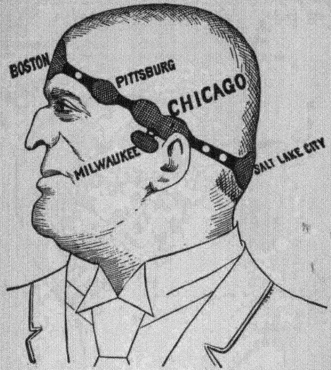

THE PSYCHOLOGICAL RAILWAY.

This road starts out from Amativeness. What faculty better represents polygamy? That is what Salt Lake City is famous for. Didn't Brigham Young live there?

Chicago's two dominant characteristics are pig-sticking and money-making. She is well represented by the two elements, Destructiveness and Acquisitiveness.

What better representative of Alimentiveness could we find in all the country than Milwaukee? Do they not **eat** and **drink** and manufacture something for others to drink up there?

Pittsburg is the best representative of Constructiveness in the United States. Can you think of Pittsburg and not think of **smoke** and **manufacturing**?

Is not Boston the **thought** center of the country? What could it think with but Comparison and Causality? It is true they cultivate Alimentiveness as well as Milwaukee, but then they only **indulge** in **beans**.

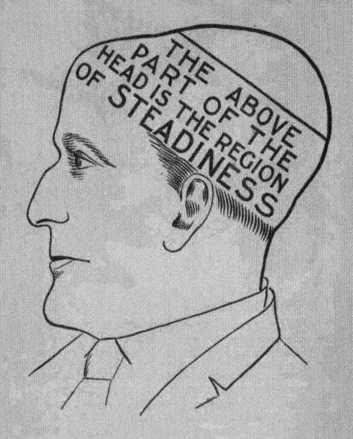

The reason this is true is because Firmness, Self-esteem and Continuity are located in the region above the line in the picture.

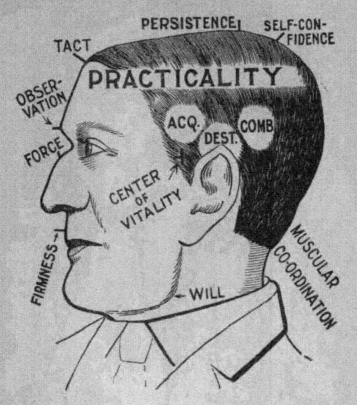

To be practical is to be able to see, handle the hands and body, tell the commercial value and courageously execute. The form of head in the above illustration has predominant the faculties that make one very practical.

WHAT MAKES ONE HANDY?

To be handy is to possess large Perceptive faculties and Constructiveness.

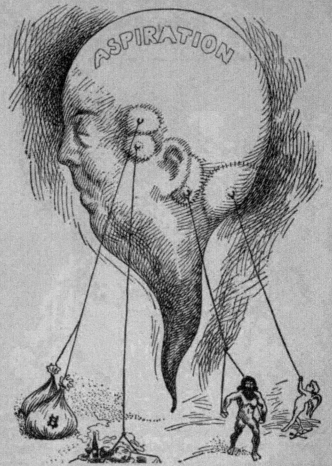

The four faculties that hold people to the earth most are Vitativeness, Amativeness, Alimentiveness and Acquisitiveness. Study this and make your own observations.

ARISTOCRACY.

Aristocracy is an assumed feeling, the specific product of Approbativeness and Self-esteem.

Here is a remarkable outline to study. The heavy outline represents a well-balanced head. The other shows very weak faculties of Benevolence, Self-esteem, Inhabitiveness and Parental Love, with enormous Amativeness. Just this much difference in the formation of a head will make two lives absolutely opposite in tendency and character.

OUT OF TUNE.

Yes out of tune. That is what is the matter with him.
His life is a miserable discord. He is out of tune and
does not know it. The world is all right, but he does not
know it. His faculties are in perpetual combat. HE
ΞDS TUNING UP.

HOW TO DETECT A FRIENDLY PERSON.

If Friendship is large the backhead will be prominent, as indicated in the above picture. The lips, if not diseased, will have distinct creases across them. They are likely to be full in size and curved instead of straight. Curved lines running around the corners of the mouth indicate positive friendship. In the handshake, friendship will manifest itself by grasping the hand warmly and shaking it heartily.

Men, women and children with this faculty strong will respond to friendly manifestations on the part of **teacher, traveler, solicitor** or **salesman** very quickly unless they have very strong Acquisitiveness, Secretiveness or Self-

esteem. These faculties make people suspicious and independent and therefore inclined to be wary of the friendly
approaches of strangers. But the manifestations of true
friendliness will overcome the most obstinate pride and
the most Indian-like suspicion if **manifested naturally
and continuously.**

The Dark parts are all that can be seen of the selfish ter-
tory from a front view.

The Location of Secretiveness with its Facial Centers.

MEMORY.

Memory is not a faculty. All faculties have their own memories, and their **conscious** memory in union with Causality, Comparison and Human Nature. **Anyone** with Eventuality, Time and Language predominant will be more inclined to merely memorize than to study and carefully examine.

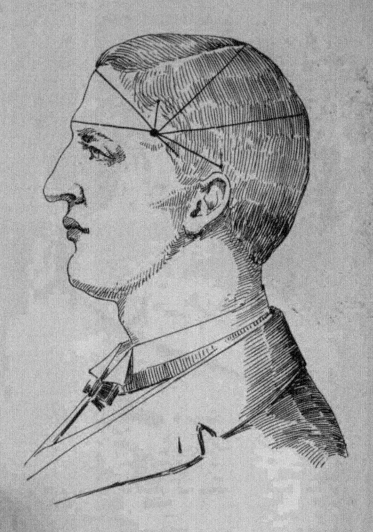

The Center of Inventive Genius.

Combativeness in Head and Face.

EFFICIENCY.

To be greatly efficient is to possess all the intellectual faculties with a strong degree of Self-esteem, Combativeness, Destructiveness and Firmness to put them into use.

The Location of Self-Esteem with its Facial Centers.

THE FACULTIES THAT HOLD THE BODY UP.

1. Firmness.
2. Self-Esteem.
3. Approbativeness.
4. Combativeness.
5. Destructiveness.
6. Amativeness.
7. Weight.

1. Amativeness.
2. Destructiveness.
3. Alimentiveness.
4. Secretiveness.
5. Acquisitiveness.
6. Mirthfulness.
7. Approbativeness.

EYE SHUTTERS.

Eyes do not close of their own accord.
They are **operated**.

They are operated by faculties. Certain faculties out of the forty-two of which the mind is composed have control of them chiefly, so far as **shutting** is concerned.

There are seven of these.

They are chiefly **selfish** in their nature.

They are self-protectors.

They look out for No. 1.

Each one of the seven has its own individual effect upon the muscles of the eyelids and brows.

Amativeness and Alimentiveness **thicken** the lids somewhat like those of a pig.

Destructiveness **straightens** the upper lid and presses it down in a **hard, horizontal** way. This faculty gives the stern, fierce, lowered expression to eyes and eyebrows.

Secretiveness "plays possum." It shuts up the eyes in a secretive, suspicious manner.

Acquisitiveness often unites with Secretiveness and makes one more suspicious, especially concerning property or money and in this way helps close the eyes.

Approbativeness causes the upper lid to somewhat droop as may be noticed in flirts and coquettes.

Mirthfulness gives a merry twinkle to the eyes by contracting the lids, and forming the lines directly outward from each corner.

Learn the location and function of these seven faculties and watch them operate the lids of the eyes, especially in "shutting up."

DON'T!

PLEASE DON'T!

Don't guess at human nature.

Don't guess at children.

Don't guess at defectives.

Don't guess at character building.

Don't guess at mental phenomena.

Don't guess at psychology.

Don't guess at **anything human.**

KNOW. **All can know by thoroughly studying the elements of human nature.**

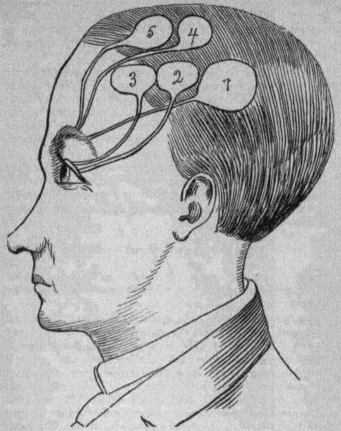

1. Cautiousness.   3. Ideality.
2. Sublimity.   4. Hope.
5. Spirituality.

EYE OPENERS.

Yes, there are natural eye openers. **Inherent** eye openers. The principal ones are Spirituality, Hope, Cautiousness, Ideality and Sublimity. These faculties have more to do with opening the eyes than all the other faculties combined.   Cautiousness will open them in fear; Ideality in viewing the beautiful; Sublimity in viewing the sublime; Hope in bright expectation; while Spirituality will cause one to stand in "open-eyed wonder."

When these five genetic faculties are predominant in one's soul make-up, they will keep his eyes open and his brows raised all of the time.   In other words, eyes and brows will be **formed** in that way.   If our readers will simply study these five faculties in action in men, women and children they will be able to positively demonstrate the truthfulness of these statements.

Select a party with either Cautiousness or Spirituality large and call the faculty into vigorous action by a picture of danger or a description of some wonderful phenomenon and the effect upon the eyes and brows will be instantaneous.

THE CRYING FACULTIES.

The two particular elements of mind that make men, women and children cry are Benevolence and Approbativeness.

Benevolence gives great susceptibility to the suffering of others, and when not regulated will start the tears very easily.   It makes children tender and easily hurt in mind and body, and gives a strong tendency to cry. Approbativeness is the sensitive faculty and comes next to Benevolence in making people cry.   It is this faculty that is hurt by neglects, slights, unkind words, criticisms and want of appreciation.   Then if one has not enough Self-esteem, he will be very easily wounded and manifest it by crying.

Add to these, strong Friendship, Conjugality, Parental Love and Inhabitiveness and one will be very susceptible to tears.

Those who do not cry very easily are endowed with predominant faculties of Destructiveness, Combativeness, Self-esteem and Firmness with the crying faculties just named weak.

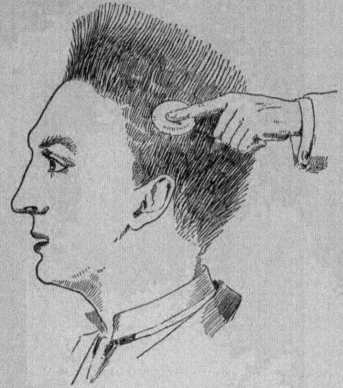

HOW TO RAISE HAIR.
Just Touch the Right Button—faculty.
GRATITUDE.

One who feels grateful for any favor has strong Benevolence and Conscientiousness. One with a weak development of these two faculties or mind elements may have all of the other faculties highly developed and manifest no gratitude. Be sure that these two faculties are very strong in one's make-up and you will be sure of gratitude. The other faculties that help these two faculties in an earnest expression of gratitude are Friendship, Parental Love, Veneration and Conjugality.

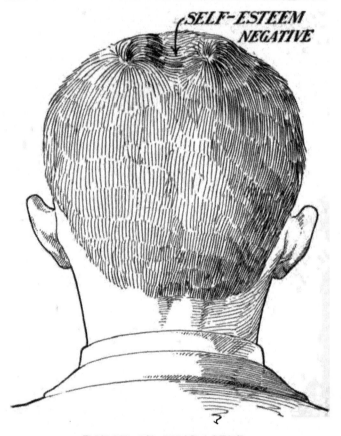

FORCE OF CHARACTER.

Force of character is elementally made up of Self-esteem, Firmness, Combativeness and Destructiveness. If it is any particular kind of force of character you have to add some other mental element. For instance, add Conscientiousness to these and you have a strong moral character. Add Acquisitiveness and you have commercial force of character. Add Causality and you get thought force of character.

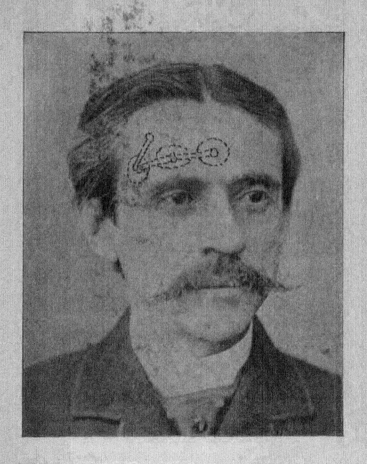

The location of Mirthfulness, Tune, Time and Eventuality.

ROBERT LOUIS STEVENSON.

Author of "Dr. Jekyll and Mr. Hyde."

THE KEYNOTE OF A GENIUS.

All the race has done has been done with the forty-two faculties that constitute the human mind.

Individual geniuses have some of these very highly developed. Their heads tell the story.

They show the **special** development and thus give us the "keynote" of their genius.

Robert Louis Stevenson's talent was of the order of genius. He **could** not have produced "Dr. Jekyll and Mr. Hyde" **without** a great development of the faculties of Form and Comparison. In a study of his head **we** were struck with the **very great** development of his faculty of Form.

The size of this faculty is indicated by width between the eyes or from pupil to pupil.

We regard this faculty as the "keynote" of the combination of faculties that produced the above-named work.

Comparison is also strikingly developed.

Faculties are related to the face through the **nervous** system. Here are four faculties connected with their facial poles and muscles. Spirituality lifts the brows. Approbativeness lifts the upper lip and exposes the teeth. Combativeness is related to the lower half of the nose. Vitativeness is related to the anterior part of the chin.

THE THOUGHT CENTERS.

The localization of the thinking faculties is very easy, and yet the majority of the human race if asked to locate them would fail. Think of a **teacher teaching without** knowing **what** the thinking faculties **are, where** they are **located** and **how** to **measure them!**

Fundamentally there is only **one thinking** faculty. This is Causality. Without this faculty there could be no thought whatever. We want each one of our readers to understand this fact in the most complete sense. The other forty-one faculties, if they were as large as they have ever been in human beings, could not originate the simplest thought ever thought. Causality is **absolutely** necessary **to any degree** or **kind** of thought whatever.

The first assistant of Causality is Comparison. This is so because a great part of thinking is comparative or analogical. These two faculties are as certainly localized as eye and nose. They occupy the brain territory **cut out** in the illustration. They are there **and never elsewhere.**

Those who do not know **exactly** where to look for these two faculties should be **infinitely pitied, very kindly held up to public ridicule, thoroughly humiliated,** and if in public positions as teachers and ministers, and **refuse to learn, severely roasted.**

GET OUT.

Get out of **thought confusion.**
Get out of **psychological mysticism.**
Get out of **educational chaos.**
Get out of **therapeutical assumption.**
Get out of **economical nonsense.**
Get out of **spiritual indefiniteness.**
Get out of **memory schemes.**
Get out of **temperamental guessing.**
Get out of **ideal delusion.**
Get out of **superficial child study.**
Get out of **theoretical speculation.**
Get out of **general uncertainty.**

You can do so by GETTING IN to your minds a **clear knowledge** of the forty-two ELEMENTS of which human minds are composed.

NO ESCAPE.

All have got to come to it. There is no escape. The **constitution of human nature** is the **standard** that all have got to come to. All theories, **isms,** and **ologies** will **necessarily** have to totter and fall when not founded upon the **constitution** of the human mind.

WHAT THE FORTY-TWO FACULTIES DO.

The forty-two human faculties do almost everything under the sun. They do everything that the race does. The range of their operations is from the highest to the lowest, from the broadest to the narrowest, and from the simplest to the most complex.

They do our thinking, talking, speaking, singing, dancing, loving, hating, swearing, fearing, walking, running, eating, grasping, working, balancing, remembering, traveling, looking, classifying, constructing, idealizing, hoping, praying, imagining, building, associating, laughing, calculating, coloring, imitating, sympathizing, persisting, combating, pushing, rustling, getting, secreting, wishing, continuing, concentrating, writing, philosophizing, reflecting, meditating, cogitating, playing, pitching, tumbling, hurling, fighting, contending, begging, resisting, lying, magnifying, exaggerating, estimating, locating, whispering, stealing, murdering, monopolizing, overcoming, crushing, determining, selecting, choosing, mastering, finishing, ordering, numbering, demonstrating, reading, spelling, writing, committing, holding, economizing, spending, wasting, dissipating, bluffing, deceiving, simulating, tyrannizing, elaborating, analyzing, synthesizing, grabbing, tasting, drinking, destroying, poisoning, burning, rhyming, picturing, illustrating, observing, marrying, fascinating, hypnotizing, attracting, affecting, modulating, emphasizing, depicting, portraying, describing, selecting, promulgating, enumerating, reviewing, soliloquizing, spiritualizing, sympathizing, helping, warring, improving, progressing, gathering, investigating, searching, applauding, criticising, denouncing, blaming, censuring.

PROUD CHARACTER.

The fundamental elements of pride are Approbativeness and Self-esteem. To understand pride is to understand these two faculties and what faculties they unite with. For instance, if one has these two faculties strong and also a strong degree of Acquisitiveness, he will have great **commercial** pride.

The dominant faculties in any race or tribe will explain the customs and productions of the tribe.

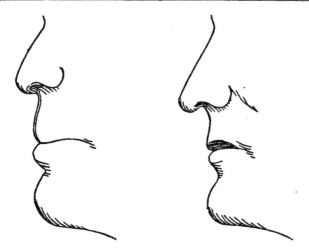

Self-esteem and Firmness
are shown in these lips.

Conjugality, Parental Love
Amativeness and Friend-
ship are shown in these.

THE AUDITORY STUDENT.

The auditory student has a predominance of Tune, Time, Ideality, Sublimity, Cautiousness, Spirituality, Veneration and Approbativeness. These make the natural listener.

THE MEMORY STUDENT.

The student who chiefly depends upon his memory has Eventuality, Language, Imitation, Tune, Time and Approbativeness in the lead in his mental make-up.

THEORETICAL.

To be theoretical in mental make-up is to have predominant faculties of Causality, Ideality and Constructiveness. Together these three faculties will spontaneously produce theory after theory and the individual fail to realize that they are only theories.

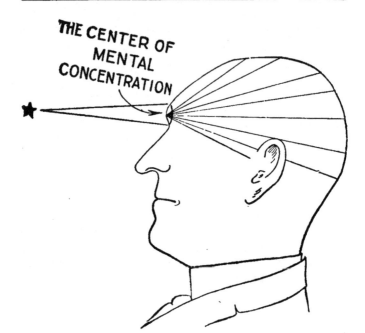

THE CENTER OF MENTAL CONCENTRATION

To focus a mind on an individual object or subject is to place the faculty of individuality in front of all the others. It is the center of mental focalization and concentration.

HOW SOME OF THE FACULTIES AFFECT THE BODY.

Friendship clings and warms the body.
Combativeness contracts the muscles and hardens the body.
Acquisitiveness grasps and pinches the body.
Benevolence sheds tears and softens the body.
Firmness stiffens and condenses the body.
Mirthfulness shakes and enlivens the body.
Veneration bows and prostrates the body.
Self-esteem bloats and holds the body erect.

**A Side View of the Faculty of Individuality, Showing a
Weak Development.**

BLUFFING.

There is much bluffing done in the world.   It is done
with Secretiveness, Human Nature, Destructiveness and
Approbativeness.   Sometimes Firmness and Self-esteem
enter into it.   One can only bluff because he is some-
what cowardly.   If Conscientiousness, Self-esteem and
Combativeness are predominant one will never bluff.
The bluffer is usually weak in all three, but especially in
Combativeness.

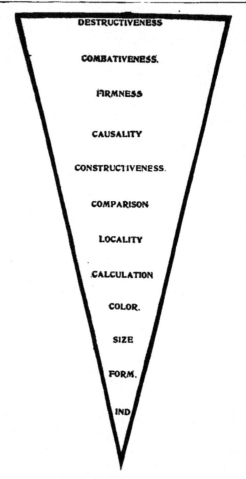

DESTRUCTIVENESS

COMBATIVENESS.

FIRMNESS

CAUSALITY

CONSTRUCTIVENESS.

COMPARISON

LOCALITY

CALCULATION

COLOR.

SIZE

FORM.

IND

AN INTELLECTUAL WEDGE.

We present above an intellectual wedge that is guaranteed to split open all knotty intellectual timber. It is a natural wedge. It is in accord with the formation of the human intellect. It is a fundamental knowledge wedge. We commend it to the educational world.

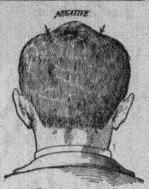

POSITIVE   *NEGATIVE*

Conscientiousness.   Conscientiousness.

RELIABILITY.

Human reliability has a center. It begins somewhere. This somewhere is the faculty of Conscientiousness. This is the center post of it. Always look
for the center post when you look for reliability in
men, women and children. There are other elements
that help make up the whole of reliable character, but
Conscientiousness is the trunk of the tree. Go directly
up from the back part of the ear and when about one
and one-half inches from the center of the head sidewise, stop, and you will be on the external location of
Conscientiousness. When positive in the character,
this part of the head will be convex in shape and when
negative concave. A neutral degree of it will be indicated by flatness. This is the only faculty of human
nature that is honest from principle. If this faculty
is weak in one, the faculties of Benevolence, Friendship,
Self-esteem, Approbativeness, Veneration and Cautiousness have to be very strong to keep one from positive dishonesty.

Special effort has been made to show the exact location of this very important element of human character and how to detect it in head, face and manner.
It gives a clear, earnest, straightforward ring to the
voice and a steady, straightforward look to the eyes.
Specially study the face and head of Judge Cooley.
He was endowed with a positive degree of this faculty.

THE ELEMENTS AND STRUCTURE OF WILL.

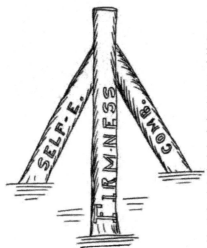

The center post of will is Firmness. Of all the faculties, this is the nearest akin to will itself. Do not misunderstand us. Will is not something in itself. It is only a **temporary state** of certain faculties in action, while faculties are permanent individual elements that **may be immortal.** Will is action, while faculty is the actor. Will may rise and fall like the tides. It is only a power of the mind—that is, of faculty. No faculty, no will.

Beginning with firmness as the **backbone** of will, we can add Combativeness, and have a **resistant** prop. These two faculties together constitute the fundamental structure of will. They give **resistant** persistence. To these two we may add Self-esteem, and give them **confidence.** Those who are positively self-confident possess one of the chief elements of will. Observe the illustration above It shows how Firmness is propped and sustained by Combativeness on one side and Self-esteem on the other.

These three faculties give us the **framework** of will. Without the other faculties these three will simply give the blind stubbornness and resistance of the **pig and mule.**

Add a strong faculty of Conscientiousness to these and you have blind moral will or persistent resistance to oppression and injustice. If Causality and Human Nature are added, then we have an intelligent moral will. In this way will can be definitely understood in any man, woman or child.

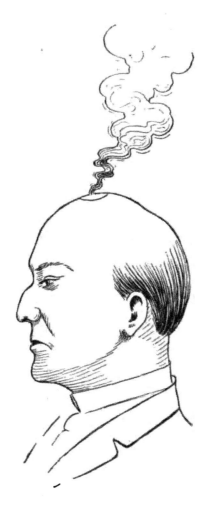

Holy Smoke.

Self Explanatory.

CENTERS OF CHARACTER.

SPECIFIC FACULTIES are the **CENTER POSTS** of distinct characteristics, talents and powers. To "hit the nail on the head," "pierce the bull's eye," and be **FUNDAMENTALLY DEFINITE** in character reading, all should understand these central faculties and not proceed in that haphazard, general, hit or miss way that is avoidable only by a **THOROUGH KNOWLEDGE** of all the

FUNDAMENTAL HUMAN FACULTIES.

Firmness is the center of **Will**.
Amativeness is the center of the **Social Evil**.
Destructiveness is the center of **Force**.
Benevolence is the center of **Humanitarianism**.
Ideality is the center of **Art**.
Acquisitiveness is the center of **Monopoly**.
Approbativeness is the center of **Jealousy**.
Eventuality is the center of **Memory**.
Causality is the center of **Thought**.
Conscientiousness is the center of Morality.
Parental Love is the center of **Parentage**.
Cautiousness is the center of **Fear**.
Human Nature is the center of **Intuition**.
Individuality is the center of **Observation**.
Constructiveness is the center of **Invention**.
Spirituality is the center of **Occultism**.
Mirthfulness is the center of **Comedy**.
Friendship is the center of **Association**.
Vitativeness is the center of **Constitution**.
Veneration is the center of **Religion**.
Tune is the center of **Music**.
Self-esteem is the center of **Personality**.

SUIT THE GESTURE TO THE FACULTY.

In elocution and oratory one should suit the gesture to the faculty. Don't make yourself ridiculous by using a gesture that belongs to Destructiveness when you are using Ideality; and for heaven's sake don't try to make one kind of gesture suit all of the faculties.

Here is another picture of a dangerous man, especially along the immoral and sensual lines.

GET RIGHT AT IT.

Don't theorize; don't speculate; don't assume. Get right at the **elements** of it. The elements of what? Of mind. Mind is an aggregation, a composition, a constitution of individual, indivisible, genetic elements. To get right at any kind of mind is to get at some of these elements. To get at fear is to get at the element of Cautiousness; to get at the social evil is to get at Amativeness; to get at jealousy is to get at Approbativeness; to get at Superstition is to get at Spirituality. To GET AT THE BODY IS TO GET AT THE PARTS OF IT. TO GET AT THE MIND IS TO GET AT THE ELEMENTS OF IT.

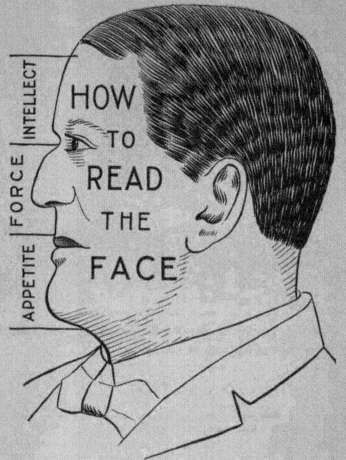

HOW TO READ THE FACE.

Faces can be read. They can be read systematically.
That is, there may be some order in physiognomy. It
has a foundation. This foundation is the mind. The
mind is made up of elements or faculties. Some of these
faculties come out in one part of the face and some in another. A fairly reliable division of three may be made.

This will cause one to look systematically at the face. While all the face included in the region of appetite in the illustration is not represented by appetite only, yet this region does **particularly** represent appetite. If it is positively predominant in the formation of the face as shown in cut No. 1, the appetites and passions will just as positively predominate in the character.

The middle division of the face represents more of the elements of force than any other part. While not all of force is shown here, it may be safely taken as the distinct region of force. If this division predominates over the one above and the one below, as illustrated in cut No. 2, force will be the dominant feature of the character.

When the highest division is the most pronounced there will be a predominance of intellect.

If the three divisions are about equal there will be a corresponding equality of the three characteristics—appetite, force and intellect. But if either positively leads, the character given and illustrated here will invariably correspond.

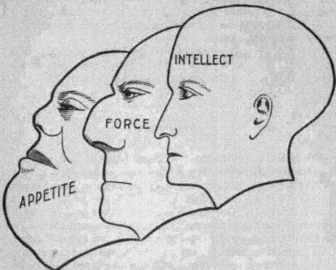

Sharply fix and compare the three faces.

INSTRUCTIVE COMPARISONS.

The faculties of the human mind may be likened,

1.   To 42 **letters**, with which one may **spell** all human tendencies, characteristics and talents.

2.   To 42 **eyes** with which one may **look into** all departments of the universe.

3.   To 42 **buds** that may **blossom** into forty-two very different flowers.   (Oh, that parents and teachers knew their blossoming **time**.)

4.   To 42 **forces** that try (and often do) **burst forth** individually.

5.   To 42 **strings** upon which are **played** all the cords and discords of human life.

6.   To 42 **factors** with which all of the problems of human life may be **solved**.

7.   To 42 **elements** out of which all mental compounds may be **made**.

8.   To 42 **figures** with which (according to permutation all of the **individuals** may be made, which clearly **accounts** for the great diversity found in the human race.

9.   To 42 **senses** with which everything objective may be **received and sensed**.

10.   To 42 **soul pieces** which **together** constitute the complex, multiplex, many-sided, self-active, self-directive, individual. indissoluble, immortal human soul.

CREDULITY.

Credulity is composed of the faculties of Spirituality, Veneration, Ideality, Sublimity and Conscientiousness. When these five faculties are predominant in one's mind he will be very credulous.   The chief one of the five is Spirituality.   There can be no credulity whatever without these faculties, and particularly without Spirituality, Conscientiousness and Ideality.   When Human Nature, Comparison, Causality and Secretiveness are weak and the above five strong, **credulity will run to seed**.   The latter four are the **antidotes** of the other five.

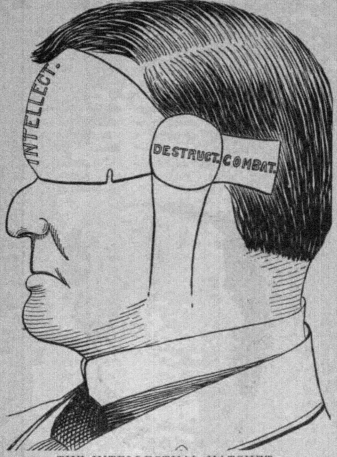

THE INTELLECTUAL HATCHET.

Intellect, however strong in itself, is **powerless** alone. One might possess the intellect of a Webster and be powerless to use this intellect **without executive force**. There is no force in intellect itself. In other words, there is no motor power in intellect. Unless there is back of intellect strong faculties of force there will be no certain aggressive, forceful application of it. Intellect may then be considered simply the blade of the hatchet. It may be very sharp; it may be ready to cut; yet it will **not** cut unless there is power to drive it.

The power back of intellect that sends it with force is chiefly to be found in two faculties. These two faculties are Destructiveness and Combativeness. Without these the intellect would not be put into positive action at all. It would not act in a forceful way. Therefore, to form an **intellectual hatchet** by which one may cut right into all of the questions of life, is to have back of it strong faculties of Destructiveness and Combativeness.

One who can do head work because he has **Causality** strongly developed.

CHARACTER IN WALKING.

Of course character comes out in the walk. The reason it comes out is because it is back of walking. Bodies do not walk about of their own accord. They are only instruments that human minds use to go to and fro. Walks vary much in the same individual. There is absolutely no fixed walk. It is true there may be a characteristic walk. This means only that the individual has a strong individuality, which in turn means simply that he has a predominance of faculties like Self-esteem, Firmness, Combativeness, Destructiveness, Causality, Human Nature and subordinate faculties of Imitation, Approbativeness and Veneration. There cannot be any positively fixed walk, for the reason that there is no positively fixed mind. Mind is not a fixed thing. In a sense it is a fixable thing. It may be fixed in a certain state for a while, and this fix thrown down and another state fixed. This all comes about because of the plurality of the faculties of which the mind is composed. Our readers should bear in mind right here that what we mean by the word mind is what is often called soul or being. Mind, being and soul are one and the same thing. The height and depth, length and breadth of a human soul is simply the degree of the various faculties of which it is composed. It cannot be any deeper than the biggest faculty. It cannot be any more shallow than the weakest faculty. The variation of these faculties in a given human being will cause corresponding variations in his walk. Faculties that take the lead in the mental states must necessarily to that degree govern the muscular system of the body by means of which he walks.

To "get a move" on oneself is to get some of the movers of the mind into action. To get a fearful move on oneself is to put Cautiousness back of the muscles. One can get over a fence and up a tree under the influence of this faculty in a hurry (with a mad bull behind him), but not in the same way that he would move when on dress parade under the faculty of Approbativeness. This is the stuck-up faculty that makes men mince their walks. It is the most mincing faculty that we have. All minced, affected walks spring from this faculty in the lead. If it is assisted by a strong faculty of Amativeness, there is an addition of riggling to mincing, and both are somewhat infected with affectation. To understand character in the walk, therefore, is to know the faculties that are in action that produce the different kinds of walks. All physical movements of a natural kind are the products of the various faculties in action. There are unsubstantial walks. They show want of force, decision, courage, confidence and self-control. In such cases the feelings predominate. If a man or woman walks under the dictation of the faculties of Firmness, Self-esteem, Conscientiousness, Human Nature, Causality, Individuality and Amativeness, he or she will have a very distinct, decided, self-reliant, positive, courageous, forceful, intelligent walk.

If they are dominated by Cautiousness, Approbativeness, Veneration and Benevolence, the walk will be of an entirely different nature. It will be of a careful, respectful, deferential, subdued kind. There will be nothing in it that is bold, positive and independent. There could not be if these four faculties predominated.

The human body then may be called a very flexible instrument in the hands of the various faculties. It is made to do all kinds of things. It has no tendencies nor desires of its own. There are, strictly speaking, no tendencies of the flesh. The body does not contain any faculties. It is only an organism through which faculties manifest themselves. The faculties have, in all normal instances complete control of it. They bend it this way and that. They simply operate it. They operate it much more successfully and freely than the engineer operates his engine. They are closer to it, by far, than any man can get to a mechanical instrument. The relation between faculties and the body are the most intimate. They have grown up together. They are far more intimately and delicately connected than were the Siamese Twins. By means of the muscular and nervous systems all kinds of movements are made.

A faculty acts. This action takes place in the brain, or, in other words, in the organs of the faculty. By means of the nervous system this action can be transmitted all over the body. When one is aroused in the faculty of Destructiveness, which is the faculty of force **per se,** this may come out in a forceful way, via the fist or foot. In other words, by means of the nerves and muscles of the arm and leg one is able to strike or kick under the dynamic force of Destructiveness. This is the center of striking, kicking, pounding, crushing force. Those who have this faculty decidedly predominant walk in a manner that can be appropriately called "the walk-right-through spirit." Every motion is forceful. "Forward" is in each motion. They go forward. They go **directly** forward. They go forward positively. They go forward somewhat as a projectile is driven by a heavy charge of powder. This can be clearly seen in the walk. The walk is not tame. It is rough. Such people will get through a crowd by "main force and awkwardness." They **drive** their bodies through. They **make** a roadway. If the perceptive faculties are strong they quickly **see** how to get through. They are quick to take advantage of an opening. They constitute a **forceful wedge.** In football the "flying wedge" is made up of such characters. All have come in contact with them, especially in crowds. On the streets of Chicago they may be met. They usually get the **right of way.** They take "bee lines" to their destination.

Combativeness has not the same driving power as Destructiveness. It comes out in a different way. It makes a different walk. It runs the body in a different manner. Instead of driving the body along forcefully it gives one an **elastic, springy** walk. Those under Combativeness are muscularly keyed up—that is, they have their muscles contracted nearly all of the time, ready for a spring or for defense. They are quicker than those under Destructiveness, so far as motion is concerned. They, however, lack the driving power. They are **resistant** in their manner and walk instead of forceful. If you crowd them they will **push back.** They do not make roadways in a crowd as do those with large Destructiveness. They have simply great **defensive** power. They walk as if they had springs in their knees. There is a crispness and a boldness that is not seen in the Destructive walk. The Destructive walk is more heavy and brutal. The Combative walk is more **fearless** and **highstrung**. The head is held a little backward as a rule when Combativeness is in the lead. When Destructiveness is in the lead, the head is held a little forward and downward. Destructiveness is a **battering-ram**. Combativeness is a **defensive armor.**

When both of these faculties are predominant in one, others may well take care. It is best that they give such the right of way.

Now, if these two faculties were subordinate in strength, and Secretiveness, Cautiousness and Acquisitiveness predominant, one would walk in a strikingly different manner. Such a person would be stealthy, watchful, careful and suspicious in his walk and manner. Very probably he would button his clothes tightly. He would have **secret pockets.** He would put his money away very carefully. He would do nothing in a loud manner. There would be no boldness in his action. He would combine the caution of woman with the stealth of the Indian and the watchfulness of the miser. This would come out in a different muscular manner. Instead of touching the heel to the floor or earth first he would be apt to touch the toes, or at least the frontal half of his feet. In fact anyone walking under the faculties of Secretiveness, Cautiousness and Acquisitiveness will walk in the most light, stealthy manner. He will **slip along.** He will feel his way by means of Cautiousness. Instead of walking right along, boldly and roughly, he will **glide** through a crowd very much in the same manner that **a snake creeps through the grass.** In fact, he has a **serpentine** walk. You never know he is coming until he is upon you. He passes before you are aware of his presence. This all comes about by means of predominant faculties.

Predominant faculties determine the characteristic walk, if any. Some one may say that it is merely a matter of habit. Very well. What is a habit but a brain state formed by the action of predominant faculties? No faculty, no habit. Something must act and act repeatedly before a habit is formed. This something is the mind as a whole. This mind is a composition of faculties. All of its acts are acts of one or more faculties. Hence, all normal physical movements are the result of **past** and **present** actions of faculties. This embodies **all training**. No one can be taught or trained except by means of faculty; we learn all that we learn with faculties. The greater share of one's training is that which comes from his own strongest faculties. He trains his arms and legs to move in certain ways by means of the inherent force of predominating faculties.

If Benevolence is supreme, his walk is positively different from another's whose Destructiveness is supreme.

The manner of **holding** the body is one thing and **moving** it another. The two together are usually called the characteristic walk of one. All should remember that we **move the body about** with certain faculties and **hold it up** with others.

We hold it up chiefly with Self-esteem, Firmness and Approbativeness. If these three faculties are weak no one will hold his body in an erect, dignified attitude. **He can not** without special effort and then only momentarily. At the same time one with these three faculties very predominant will hold the body in a swaggering, pompous position of vanity and ostentation, and with the addition of strong Destructiveness and Combativeness he will push along boldly, independently and powerfully.

The faculties that move the body about chiefly are Destructiveness and Combativeness.

The particular manner of movement is determined by any of the other faculties that may be strong enough to do so. It will be moved according to the nature and relative strength of the **movers**. If Ideality is strong it will cause the owner to **try** to walk **gracefully** as well as pompously and boldly. A large faculty of Hope will give the walk a cheerful air. Mirthfulness will saturate it with the jolly or droll.

In this way all kinds of normal human walks may be very clearly read and understood.

NERVOUSNESS.

Mental nervousness all comes from two faculties—Approbativeness and Cautiousness. None of the other elements of mind has any ability to feel nervous. To be afraid in any degree in any kind of way is to be so either from the inherent nature of these two faculties or by means of some other faculites, uniting with these. Some degree then of one of these two mind elements is absolutely necessary to any mental nervousness. What we mean is that all fear of criticism, ridicule condemnation, failure, disease and death are the products of these two elements.

HOW SOME OF THE FACULTIES WRITE.

Styles of handwriting can be traced directly to **individual** faculties. We have been aware of this for many years and have positively demonstrated it in many cases. Action and motion have their sources in human faculties. If one has in tact all his bones and muscles, his writing will truthfully represent the faculties that **dictate** his writing and their degree of culture.

Benevolence

Take predominating Benevolence and it will have enough influence over the other faculties to write as you see in the figure. Compare with the signatures of Lincoln and Longfellow, two truly benevolent men.

Acquisitiveness

When Acquisitiveness is predominant you do not see so much generous use of space nor the smooth, drooping curve of kindness. Acquisitiveness likes to economize space as well as property.

Cautiousness is careful.   It will be more careful in crossing its t's and dotting its i's.   It helps to make legibility.

Approbativeness is the great displayer.   It spoils a great deal of writing.   Notice the illustration closely and then call to mind acquaintances who are very strong in this faculty and therefore fond of display and you will see the similarity quickly.

Anybody who writes this way is subject to **flattery**. Remember that Approbativeness is the **center** of flattery. It is the only faculty that likes it.

Don't give yourself away in your writing, **particularly your weakness.**

Impulsive Lips.

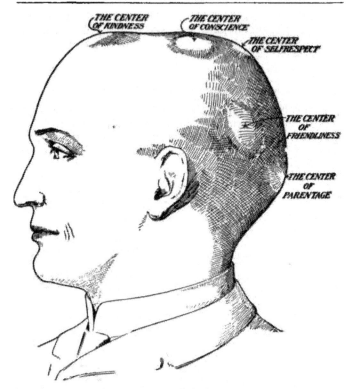

It will decidedly pay all to localize these elements and make use of this knowledge.

WHERE VOICES COME FROM.

Affectionate voices always come from the backhead.

Heavy, thunderous voices always come from the sidehead.

Egotistical voices come from the crown of the head.

Kind, respectful and straightforward voices come from the tophead.

All voices are produced by the forty-two mental elements.

WHILE ASLEEP.
The Best Time to Reconstruct the Brain.

Brain grows principally at night. In other words, it grows while a child is **asleep**. Dreams can be regulated. They can be used to great advantage in child culture. The brain is a very composite organ. There are two organs for each faculty, one in each hemisphere. Faculties differ so much in size in a given child that some become decidedly too strong for the others.

Suppose a child has at birth a strong faculty of Destructiveness. This can be quite easily located by pressing the frontal part of the tips of the two ears against the head. When this locality rounds out or shows a distinct convexity of form the organs of Destructiveness are large. Unless a child has the **counteracting** faculty of Benevolence to a large degree it will become very rough and even fierce and revengeful in disposition. To counteract this too active condition of Destructiveness is to **keep** or **take** the **blood** away from it as much as possible. The blood goes to that part of the brain most in which the largest faculties are located because these are the most active and demand the most blood.

Parents and teachers may very certainly take the overstock of blood away from the two organs of Destructiveness by relating something that is very pathetic **immediately** before a vicious child goes to sleep, for in this way the blood may be centered in the organs of Benevolence to that degree that the dreams may be largely regulated and even determined in advance. This has been proven by actual tests.

Never let a revengeful child go to sleep in anger. Always take the blood largely out of the organs of Destructiveness by **vigorously calling into action** any of the counteracting faculties of this faculty, as Friendship, Benevolence, Cautiousness, Conscientiousness. This can be done by parents who understand the forty-two faculties of which all children's minds are constituted. It can be done as **certainly** as they can have a child use **one arm** specially in some vigorous exercise before retiring. **General experimenting** in child culture, is **no longer necessary**.

POINTED POINTS ABOUT CHARACTER READING.

A large head does not always indicate a large brain. The size may be made up largely of hair, scalp, fatty tissue and skull.

Phrenology has been blamed for a great many deformed heads. A head that has been deformed at birth phrenology is not responsible for. A little learning is a dangerous thing right here.

A one-sided view of a human head is not nearly reliable, so far as honesty is concerned. A head may be beautifully symmetrical from the nape of the neck to the root of the nose from a side view, and at the same time be roof shaped when looked at from a front view. Such heads are not necessarily honest, spiritual nor moral.

To read human character definitely, is to understand the human faculties, and measure each one as it is developed in the brain. Human Anatomy is largely reliable, because the different parts of it can be definitely located. Phrenology is reliable as an art for the same reason.

The sources and causes of all kinds of human manifestations can only be found in **elementary** faculties. To attempt to read human character without directly measuring faculty is, at the most, experimental general work.

Faculties come out so that all who will make the effort can see them. They come out externally in the formation of the head. They come out facially in distinct parts of the face. They come out motionally in distinct walks and gestures. They come out vocally in distinct tones of voice.

HEAD WORK.

Head workers are very easily picked out. To do headwork to any degree whatever is to possess some degree of the faculties of Causality and Constructiveness. No other faculties have any power to do any head work; in other words, no planning, thinking, originating talent is possible without some degree of these faculties.

In selecting men and women for head work be sure they have these two faculties quite well developed.

THE UTILITY OF BALD HEADS.

One class of bald heads tower very high right up from the backs of the ears.   They run up to a peak.   This means a strong degree of Firmness.   It is likely to mean obstinacy.   If the whole crown of the head is rounded out, including this high peak, one will be positively domineering in disposition.

Any young woman who marries a young man or a man with a bald head like this will find that she has a very domineering, egotistical character to deal with.

If this region of the head is very deficient, one will be correspondingly deficient in self-reliance, persistence and ambition.   Such may have excellent talent, but not the determination and confidence to put it into execution.

By means of bald heads one may quickly determine to a great degree whether a man is feminine or masculine. If he is higher in the frontal part of the tophead than the crown he has more tenderness than self will and is therefore more feminine than masculine so far as these characteristics are concerned.   Complete masculine heads always tower very high in the crown.   In fact, that is their highest part.   Feminine heads are higher in the frontal part of the tophead than in the crown.   This will give our readers an idea of the great practical utility of bald heads.   Make use of them.   They can be used for the best scientific purposes and we hope all will very respectfully do so.

CHARACTER IN VOICE.

Character makes voice. In other words, faculties make voice.

An **affectionate** voice is made by Friendship, Conjugality, Amativeness and Parental Love.

An **affected** voice is made by Approbativeness.

A **self-important** voice is made by Self-esteem and Approbativeness.

A **decided** voice is made by Firmness, Combativeness and Self-esteem.

An **earnest** voice is made by Conscientiousness, Benevolence, Friendship, Conjugality and Veneration.

A **kind** voice is made by Benevolence.

A **genuine** voice is made by Conscientiousness.

A **pleasant** voice is made by Benevolence, Friendship, Veneration, Conscientiousness, Approbativeness and Suavity.

A **gruff** voice is made by Destructiveness and Self-esteem.

A **musical** voice is made by Tune, Time, Ideality and strong social and moral sentiments.

A **deceitful** voice is made by Secretiveness, Amativeness, Approbativeness, Acquisitiveness and Human Nature.

Watch the human faculties in action and you can prove this for yourself.

LOCALIZATION.

The localization of the organs of the forty-two faculties is just as true as the localization of the ear, the nose, the heart, the lungs, the stomach, or any and all of the organs of the body.   This localization is just as **natural.** In fact, it is absolutely natural.

Man had nothing whatever to do with localization. He simply discovered it.   Phrenologists have had no more to do with the location of the faculties than with the location of the organs of the body.   They simply. found the faculties.   The location of a faculty can be mastered and depended upon as certainly as the location of the ear.   Even a child knows where to look for his ears.   The location of Causality, Benevolence, Destructiveness, Cautiousness and Amativeness can be learned and depended upon just as certainly and absolutely as the location of the nose can be learned and depended upon.   It would be a very unreliable geography of this country that could not be depended upon if one wanted to locate New York, Boston, Philadelphia, St. Louis, Cincinnati and Pittsburg.   These cities are located somewhere.   They are there all the time.   They can be found.   This location, the geography of the United States furnishes one.   The **geography of the' human head** may be just as certainly learned.   It can be depended upon with just as much certainty.   And it is a great deal more important than the geography of any country.

HOW CAN ONE BE QUICK?

To be quick is to have a predominant degree of Combativeness, Human Nature, Individuality, Self-esteem, Firmness, Eventuality, Destructiveness, Weight, Amativeness, Comparison and Language.

These faculties give quick observation, quick movements, quick decision, quick expression, quick memory and quick thought.   Then, when the slow faculties— Cautiousness, Causality, Approbativeness, Conscientiousness, Order, Ideality, Continuity, Veneration—are weak, one will be very quick.

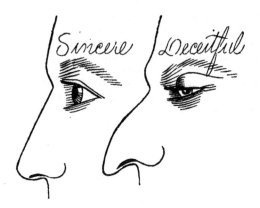

EASILY UPSET.

Many people are easily **upset.** They get "rattled" easily. They lose "presence of mind." They "fly off the handle." They "lose their grip." Why? Because they have **a** weak development of **certain** fundamental faculties whose business is to give one **self-control.** We say **certain** faculties purposely. **Only** certain faculties possess the power to give one self-control. They give one this power by virtue of their **nature.** It can come from no other source. If these faculties are not **strongly developed**, no one on earth will have self-control. These faculties are Self-esteem, Combativeness, Causality, Conscientiousness, Human Nature, Firmness, and sometimes Spirituality and Destructiveness.

Without these eight faculties, self-control would be as impossible as locomotive engineering without an engineer. When these faculties are strong enough as members of the **mental constitution** there will be self-control in any **man, woman** or **child.**

No one can be **upset** with these faculties **predominant.** They can be **cultivated** when they are too weak.

THE SELECTION OF EMPLOYES.

For handiwork select those with large perceptive faculties and rather broad heads.

For head work select those with good upper foreheads that are rather square.

For salesmen get broad heads, full eyes and those who have the faculty of Human Nature very strong.

For superintendents get those with broad heads, high in the crown and good foreheads.

For hustlers always get those with broad heads and high in the crown.

For all kinds of honest employes be sure to get those with high, broad topheads and full upper backheads.

Master everything in this book and you will be able to select just the kind of employe you want.

HOW MUCH?

How much science of music would there be without any notes? How much science of arithmetic without any figures? How much science of chemistry without any elements? There would be just as little science in the above mentioned as there is to-day in all psychology, education, elocution, and mental therapeutics, not founded upon the elements of the human mind.

WHEN YOU GET TIRED FLOPPING ROUND.

Teachers, Preachers, Psychologists, and all, when you get tired of stumbling and grumbling, changing and guessing and tumbling; just build on the **mental constitution** and your building will not fall.

The Composite of the Ten Selfish Faculties, Showing them Predominant in Head and Face.

WHERE TO LOOK.

The place to look for educational systems and human philosophy is in the **mental constitution** of man. The truth is inherent in this constitution.

WAYWARD CHILDREN.

Wayward children are weak in Veneration and Conscientiousness and strong in Firmness, Amativeness, Combativeness and Destructiveness.

The light part of the back head indicated here represents the location of the higher affections. The other
light part shows the location of the moral, esthetic and
reasoning faculties. Always look for the kind of elements where they belong.

MIMICRY.

The disposition and ability to mimic come from the
faculties of Mirthfulness, Human Nature and Imitation.
Then if Self-esteem, Veneration and Conscientiousness
are rather weak, one will delight in mimicing others.
To imitate dialects Tune and Language must be added.

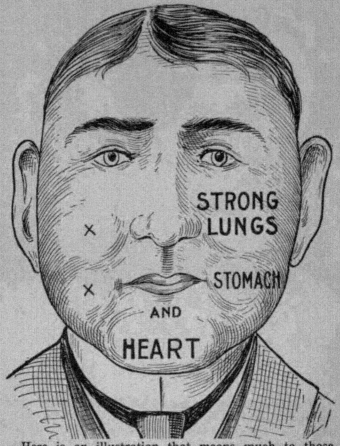

Here is an illustration that means much to those who would measure vitality and understand health. The facial lung pole is outward from the wings of the nose and indicated by a positive convexity. The digestive center is outward from the lips and indicated in the same way. A strong heart is indicated by a large, broad, projecting chin. The opposite of these developments means a negative condition of the lungs, stomach and heart.

A hand without a finger.

Anatomy without a bone.

Language without a word.

Chemistry without an element.

Music without a note.

Arithmetic without a figure.

Physiology without an organ.

Theology, psychology, sociology, criminology and anthropology without a faculty are not any more complete and useful than the above, in the condition stated.

HOW WE GET RATTLED.

All things have specific beginnings. The mental state that is denominated "rattled" can come about only by the action of one or more of three faculties—Conscientiousness, Approbativeness and Cautiousness. We get "rattled" from a sense of guilt when it is suddenly presented to us by means of Conscientiousness; this is not a frequent condition, however. We get "rattled" by fear when Cautiousness is suddenly excited. The majority, however, get "rattled" by an intense, overwhelming action of Approbativeness. This is the dominant faculty in the majority of cases of "rattles." It is that faculty that embarrasses one principally. It is the most confusing, faculty when excited, that we have. To lose self-possession is to principally let this faculty dominate one. When the three together positively predominate one is very easily "rattled." He is easily excited and confused by means of Conscientiousness and Approbativeness if he simply imagines that another thinks he is guilty. Cautiousness is apt to aggravate the case. All can rest assured that these three faculties are the only ones that will "rattle" one. To regulate them properly is to possess or cultivate to a predominant degree the faculties of Causality, Human Nature, Firmness. Self-esteem and Combativeness

FIRMNESS IN HEAD AND FACE.

The above illustration shows the location of the six elements of human goodness. These are wholly good because they desire the welfare of others, and have no selfish axes to grind. They are Parental Love, Conjugality, Friendship, Conscientiousness, Veneration and Benevolence. They exalt human nature and lift men and women into the sphere of disinterested goodness. These elements can be found nowhere else. Without them mankind would be absolutely selfish.

Can you unlock it? Do you know the names of the
doors of the human mind? Remember that you must
have a different key for each door. One mind key will
not unlock another door of this mind building.

LOOK FOR FACULTIES.

Do you know where to look for one's ears? Then you
should know where to look for one's faculties. Faculties
are not like fleas. You can put your fingers **on** them
if you know where to look for them, and if you do not
know you ought to feel so ashamed of your ignorance
that you cannot sleep well till you learn where they are.
Anyone who would be ashamed to not know where his
nose is, should be exceedingly more ashamed to not know
where his faculty of Destructiveness is. **Learn the localization of the faculties** and then when you look at a
head you will see something more than hair, scalp, scars,
indentations, lumps and sutures.

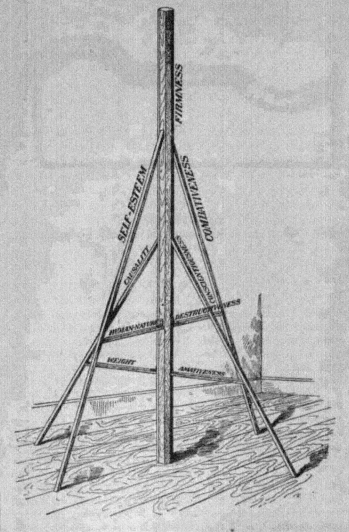

The framework of human character. Study it.

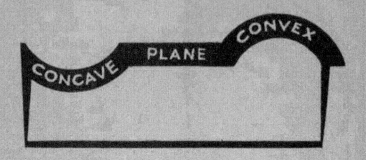

A NATURAL SCALE.
Based upon the Three Natural Principles of Formation, to wit Convex, Plane, Concave.

Each of the forty-two faculties uses two brain organs. Both of the brains, the big brain and the little brain, or the cerebrum and the cerebellum, are **double**. The sense of hearing has **two end organs**,—the two ears. The sense of vision has **two end organs**,—the eyes. There are not two **senses** of vision nor two senses of hearing. Each simply has a double apparatus through which it can perform its function. **The same is true of the forty-two human faculties.** The **organs of** these faculties are **definitely** localized. They are just as definitely located as the eyes and ears. They are just as real. How to measure them is **seemingly** the most difficult thing. The difficulty is largely in the seeming, however. They **can** be measured. The reason they can be measured is because they **constitute** the **external** convolutions of the brain. These convolutions determine the **shape** and **size** of the head. The way this comes about is like this: The forty-two faculties are usually inherited in different degrees of strength. Some are positive and some are neutral and some are negative. In other words, some are very strong, others fairly strong and others quite weak. All the positive faculties build corresponding positive

organs. The positive organs always come to the surface.
They not only come to the surface but project themselves. In shape they grow into **convexity** of form.
This is a universal law. Everything that is **positive** becomes **convex** in form. Convexity of form, therefore, is
universally indicative of a **positive** power back of it. It
could not take the convex form without this positive
power back of it. A positive faculty, therefore, builds
positive brain organs which **necessarily** become convex
in form. Above the brain organs is **the skull**, which in
every healthy, natural case is simply a protective **covering** of the brain. In a healthy child, man, or woman it
exactly conforms to the brain. It is the servant of the
brain. It does not grow into any shape **of its own accord.** There is no hereditary design in it. It is simply
formed according to the **needs** of the brain beneath it.
If there is a positive faculty, there will be positive brain
organs, and these positive brain organs take convex
forms, and above these convex brain organs there will
be skull **formations** that are correspondingly convex.
If this special faculty is very positive the brain organs
will **necessarily** be the same, and if the adjacent faculties
are neutral or negative the external head over the organs
will be flat, and hence the positive organs will stand out
boldly in a convex form simply because they are so much
stronger than the surrounding organs. If an adjacent
faculty is negative, there will be a negative development
of its brain organs, which will fail to come to the surface
of the brain in the round, convex way that positive organs
do, and hence will fail to build convex formations of
skull above. Instead there will be distinct concavities.
Natural concavities, then, are universally indicative of
negative faculties. If any faculty is simply neutral in
strength it will build brain organs that are correspondingly neutral. Above this the skull will be plane. It
will be neither convex nor concave. These three principles will explain completely all kinds of head shapes.
If all of the forty-two elements are positive, they will
build positive organs, which results in a convex skull
all **around.** If one group of faculties is positive it will

build that part of the brain that it inhabits correspondingly strong.   This may be the social faculties in the pos-
terior lobes, the selfish faculties in the temporal lobes,
the intellectual faculties in the frontal, or the moral faculties in the coronal.   When this is true there will be
one section of the external head that is convex and which
stands out boldly.   The unequal degree of the forty-two
faculties is therefore the cause of the **unequal** formation
of the **brain** and **skull.**   There is no other **natural** cause.
Head shapes, then, are absolutely, when natural, the **products** of the **various faculties.**

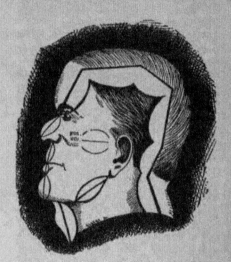

Cut Illustrating the Three Principles.

THE GREATEST REPRESENTATIVES OF
INDIVIDUAL FACULTIES.

' The forty-two men and women named below represent the strongest degree of each human faculty so far manifested by the human race.

To give our readers a pointed illustration of the highest or strongest development of an individual faculty in the human race, we have sought to find men and women who have been so predominantly endowed with a single faculty that it determined their genius.

Amativeness . . . . Brigham Young
Conjugality . . . . Mrs. W. E. Gladstone
Parental Love . . . . Frederick Froebel
Inhabitiveness . . . . John Howard Payne
Continuity . . . . Herbert Spencer
Combativeness . . . . Admiral Dewey
Destructiveness . . . . Sitting Bull
Secretiveness . . . . Aaron Burr
Cautiousness . . . . Gen. Geo. B. McClellan
Alimentiveness . . . . Roman Emperor Vitellius
Calculation . . . . Zerah Colburn
Color . . . . Rubens
Weight . . . . Blondin
Form . . . . Michael Angelo
Order. . . . . George Bancroft
Constructiveness . . . . Thomas A. Edison
Locality . . . . Christopher Columbus
Time . . . . Alexander Pope
Tune . . . . Beethoven
Eventuality . . . . Thomas Babbington Macauley
Comparison . . . . Henry Ward Beecher
Causality . . . . Daniel Webster
Mirthfulness . . . . Mark Twain
Sublimity . . . . William Cullen Bryant
Human Nature . . . . Shakespeare
Imitation . . . . Blind Tom
Benevolence . . . . Florence Nightingale
Spirituality . . . . Emanuel Swedenborg

Conscientiousness . . . . Abraham Lincoln
Firmness . . . . Prince Bismarck
Self-esteem . . . . Roscoe Conkling
Approbativeness . . . . Napoleon
Individuality . . . . Charles Darwin
Language . . . . Max Muller
Hope . . . . Ella Wheeler Wilcox
Vitativeness . . . . John Tanner
Size . . . . William Herschell
Acquisitiveness . . . . J. Pierpont Morgan
Friendship . . . . James G. Blaine
Ideality . . . . Edgar Allen Poe
Veneration . . . . Jonathan Edwards
Suavity . . . . Lord Chesterfield

ESPECIALLY WATCH THE TOPHEAD.

No human being without a good tophead need ever claim to be honest, kind, religious, moral, spiritual or philanthropical. So in every case, whether it be in business, love or church, if anyone claims to be good, generous, honest, sincere and trustworthy, you may put it down as an absolute fact that he is a hypocrite unless he has a full tophead. One cannot get something from nothing.

LIARS.

Liars lie by means of certain faculties, and always so.

The positive lying faculties are Approbativeness, Sublimity and Secretiveness. These faculties, unless governed, will instinctively stretch the truth. They will exaggerate. They will not tell a lie of their own accord of a mean, selfish, vicious kind, but will simply lie for fun and from an innate desire to exaggerate. These three faculties are the chief ones in the "sea-serpent," "big fish," "big snake," "big battle" and all kinds of colossal lying.

THE ELEMENTAL FACULTIES DEFINED.

INDIVIDUALITY:	An elemental faculty that perceives the individual existence of things and thoughts.
FORM:	An elemental faculty that perceives shapes.
SIZE:	An elemental faculty that perceives dimensions.
COLOR:	An elemental faculty that perceives colors.
EVENTUALITY:	An elemental faculty that notices events.
TIME:	An elemental faculty that watches time as it passes.
TUNE:	An elemental faculty that senses the concord of sound waves.
NUMBER:	An elemental faculty that perceives number.
ORDER:	An elemental faculty that likes orderly arrangement of things.
WEIGHT:	An elemental faculty that senses the attraction of an object to the center of the earth.
COMPARISON:	An elemental faculty that compares thoughts and things.
SPIRITUALITY:	An elemental faculty that senses that which is spiritual.
HOPE:	An elemental faculty of cheerfulness.
APPROBATIVENESS:	An elemental faculty that seeks the praise of others.
SELF-ESTEEM:	An elemental faculty that esteems self.
FIRMNESS:	An elemental faculty that persists.

CONSCIENTIOUSNESS: An elemental faculty that likes right and truth.

CONTINUITY: An elemental faculty that desires to continue that which the other faculties have started.

INHABITIVENESS: An elemental faculty that loves the place where one lives.

FRIENDSHIP: An elemental faculty that forms friendships.

CONJUGALITY: An elemental faculty that loves one.

PARENTAL LOVE An elemental faculty that loves babies.

CAUSALITY: An elemental faculty that conceives the cause and effect relations between things.

IDEALITY: An elemental faculty that perceives beauty.

HUMAN NATURE: An elemental faculty that perceives character.

VITATIVENESS: An elemental faculty that gives an inherent desire to live.

COMBATIVENESS: An elemental faculty that combats opposition.

DESTRUCTIVENESS: An elemental faculty of forceful action.

SECRETIVENESS: An elemental faculty that likes to hide thoughts and things.

CAUTIOUSNESS: An elemental faculty that feels fear.

ALIMENTIVENESS: An elemental faculty that enjoys eating.

ACQUISITIVENESS: An elemental faculty that desires to possess property of some kind.

BENEVOLENCE: An elemental faculty that sympathizes with suffering.

VENERATION: An elemental faculty that worships.

AMATIVENESS: An elemental faculty that
                      gives amative love of the op-
                      posite sex.
SUBLIMITY: An elemental faculty that
                      senses grandeur.
IMITATION: An elemental faculty that de-
                      sires to imitate.
SUAVITY: An elemental faculty that
                      gives the suave feeling.
MIRTHFULNESS: An elemental faculty that
                      senses the comical.
CONSTRUCTIVENESS: An elemental faculty that
                      gives the idea of construction.
LANGUAGE: An elemental faculty that
                      likes words.
LOCALITY: An elemental faculty that
                      perceives location.

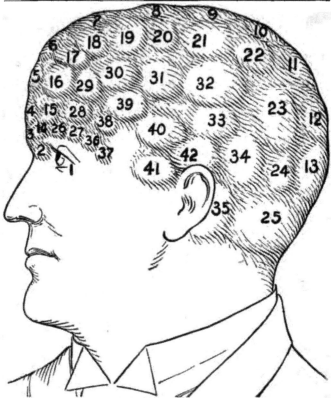

1. Language. 2. Form. 3. Individuality. 4. Eventuality. 5. Comparison. 6. Human Nature. 7. Benevolence. 8. Veneration. 9. Firmness. 10. Self-esteem. 11. Continuity. 12. Inhabitiveness. 13. Parental Love. 14. Size. 15. Locality. 16. Causality. 17. Suavity. 18. Imitation. 19. Spirituality. 20. Hope. 21. Conscientiousness. 22. Approbativeness. 23. Friendship. 24. Conjugality. 25. Amativeness. 26. Weight. 27. Color. 28. Time. 29. Mirthfulness. 30. Ideality. 31. Sublimity. 32. Cautiousness. 33. Secretiveness. 34. Combativeness; 35. Vitativeness. 36. Order. 37. Number. 38. Tune. 39. Constructiveness. 40. Acquisitiveness. 41. Alimentiveness. 42. Destructiveness.

SOME INSTRUCTION IN REGARD TO THE EX-
TERNAL LOCATION OF THE EIGHTY-
FOUR ORGANS OF THE FORTY-
TWO FACULTIES.

The lowest faculty in position is Amativeness.   This
is located in the cerebellum and can easily be detected
externally.   Start directly backward from the orifice
of the ear and about one inch back of the bone behind
the ear you, as a rule, find the location of Amativeness.
There is often a fissure that can be seen and felt immediately above it.   This is the external indication of
the separation between the cerebellum and the cerebrum.   Amativeness is also on each side of the occipital
protuberance that may be seen or felt on the lower
backhead of many.

The center of Parental Love is about one inch above
this occipital protuberance and on a horizontal line
from the tip of the ear back.

Inhabitiveness is immediately above Parental Love
and directly below the suture, perceptible on many
heads, that unites the occipital bone and the two
parietal bones.   Observe closely some man with a
bald head and you can see this distinctly.

Immediately on each side of Inhabitiveness and just
where the backhead rounds off forward and backward
is the location of Friendship.

Immediately below Friendship on each side of Parental Love and directly above the center of Amativeness, is the location of Conjugality.

Directly behind your ears, under or internal from
the mastoid bones, is the location of Vitativeness.

About one and one-half inches from the center of
the tip of the ear backward is the location of Combativeness.

Press the tips of the ears against the head and you
are upon the location of Destructiveness.

A little lower and in front of Destructiveness, and
directly above the zygomatic arch, which can be distinctly seen and felt, is the location of Alimentiveness.
It corresponds in location with the upper fourth of the
ear and about three-fourths of an inch forward.

Directly above Alimentiveness, approximately an inch, is the center of Acquisitiveness.

Directly backward from this and above Destructiveness, only a little farther back, is Secretiveness.

Immediately above Secretiveness on the corners of the head is the location of Cautiousness. The men can locate this by remembering, when it is large, where a stiff hat pinches their heads most.

Directly up from this sufficiently to be over the curve and on the side of the tophead is the location of Conscientiousness.

Directly backward and over the curve of the head is the location of Approbativeness.

About one inch from the center of Approbativeness toward the center of the head is the location of Self-esteem.

Continuity is directly downward toward Inhabitiveness, while Firmness is directly forward and upward. Continuity, however, is above the suture that is often found between it and Inhabitiveness.

To help locate Firmness, draw a straight line up from the back part of the ear to the center of the tophead and you will be on the center of it as a rule.

Direcly forward of Firmness, filling out the center of the tophead sidewise and lengthwise, forming the central part of the arch, is Veneration.

On each side of Veneration, only a little backward and directly in front of Conscientiousness, is Hope.

An inch forward of Hope and on each side of the frontal part of Veneration is Spirituality.

Directly in front of Spirituality is Imitation.

Directly toward the center from Imitation forward of Veneration and cornering with Spirituality is Benevolence.

Directly forward of Benevolence, just where the head curves off to begin the forehead, is Human Nature.

On each side of Human Nature directly in front of Imitation is Suavity.

Directly downward from Suavity causing a square formation of the forehead is Causality.

Between the two organs of Causality in the center of the upper forehead is the location of Comparison.

Directly downward from Comparison in the very center of the forehead is Eventuality.

Below Eventuality covering the two inner corners of the brows is the location of Individuality.

Directly below this, causing great width between the eyes, is the location of Form.

On each side of Form, indicated by projecting or protruding eyes, is the location of Language.

Directly outward from the corner of the eye is the location of Number.

Under the corner of the brow and directly above Number is the location of Order.

An half an inch along the brow from Order toward the center of the forehead and directly above the outer part, of the pupil of the eye is Color.

Between Color and Weight there is a little notch that runs diagonally upward, which should not be taken for a deficient faculty. Weight is on the inside of this and above the inner part of the pupil of the eye.

Size may be found directly between Weight and the faculty of Individuality, which has already been located.

Locality is diagonally up from the location of Size.

Time may be found immediately over Color, outward from Locality and a little higher, and under the outer part of Causality and the inner part of Mirthfulness.

Tune is directly outward from *Time and over the ridge that may be found on the majority of angular craniums and upward and inward from Calculation and Order.

Directly above Tune, slightly inward, is the location of Mirthfulness.

Directly back of Tune, filling out the middle of the side temple, is the location of Constructiveness.

Immediately above Constructiveness, rounding off the head toward Imitation and Spirituality, is Ideality.

Directly back of Ideality, over Acquisitiveness and in front of Cautiousness, is the location of Sublimity.

This instruction, with a thorough study of the location of the organs indicated upon the model head, will enable you to approximate their location.

DEALING WITH YOURSELF.

Reader, to deal with yourself is to deal with forty-two faculties. To handle yourself is to handle forty-two faculties. To develop yourself is to develop some of these forty-two faculties with others. To deal with yourself definitely is to understand each faculty of which you are composed. To deal with your passions is to understand whence these passions spring. To deal with your despondencies is to understand the faculties that cause despondency. To deal with your fears definitely and effectively is to understand the faculties from whence they come. To deal with your imagination, is to understand the sources of imagination, which may be found in elemental faculties. To deal with your thoughts is to understand the thought faculties and the faculties that stimulate these to action. When you fully understand the exact nature of each faculty you can definitely and successfully deal with yourself. Not understanding these elemental faculties of which you are composed and the degree in which you possess these individually and relatively is to deal with yourself blindly, vaguely, uncertainly and unsuccessfully. If you are to deal with yourself in the way that results in happiness, health and success, you must deal understandingly with all the faculties that constitute you. Study the nature of each faculty. Master these elements that constitute you. Know exactly the causes of all of your mental moods. In this way you can begin to rectify all unhappy conditions. You can correct any defect of memory, concentration, thought, judgment, will, decision or self-reliance in the most definite and certain manner.

A MENTAL INVENTORY.

FOR THE USE OF EXAMINERS.

Showing the Positive, Neutral or Negative State of
Each of the Forty-Two Faculties of which
One is Composed.

Amativeness:	Positive	Neutral	Negative
Conjugality:	Positive	Neutral	Negative
Parental Love:	Positive	Neutral	Negative
Friendship:	Positive	Neutral	Negative
Inhabitiveness:	Positive	Neutral	Negative
Continuity:	Positive	Neutral	Negative
Vitativeness:	Positive	Neutral	Negative
Combativeness:	Positive	Neutral	Negative
Destructiveness:	Positive	Neutral	Negative
Alimentiveness:	Positive	Neutral	Negative
Acquisitiveness:	Positive	Neutral	Negative
Secretiveness:	Positive	Neutral	Negative
Cautiousness:	Positive	Neutral	Negative
Approbativeness:	Positive	Neutral	Negative
Self-esteem:	Positive	Neutral	Negative
Firmness:	Positive	Neutral	Negative
Conscientiousness:	Positive	Neutral	Negative
Hope:	Positive	Neutral	Negative
Spirituality:	Positive	Neutral	**Negative**
Veneration:	Positive	**Neutral**	**Negative**

Benevolence:	Positive	Neutral	Negative
Constructiveness:	Positive	Neutral	Negative
Ideality:	Positive	Neutral	Negative
Sublimity:	Positive	Neutral	Negative
Imitation:	Positive	Neutral	Negative
Mirthfulness:	Positive	Neutral	Negative
Individuality:	Positive	Neutral	Negative
Form:	Positive	Neutral	Negative
Size:	Positive	Neutral	Negative
Weight:	Positive	Neutral	Negative
Color:	Positive	Neutral	Negative
Order:	Positive	Neutral	Negative
Number:	Positive ·	Neutral	Negative
Locality:	Positive	Neutral	Negative
Eventuality:	Positive	Neutral	Negative
Time:	Positive	Neutral	Negative
Tune:	Positive	Neutral	Negative
Language:	Positive	Neutral	Negative
Causality:	Positive	Neutral	Negative
Comparison:	Positive	Neutral	Negative
Human Nature:	Positive	Neutral	Negative
Suavity:	Positive	Neutral	Negative

PORTS OF ENTRY ON THE
SEA OF LIFE.

ARTISTIC
- Sculptor
- Designer
- Draughtsman
- Photographer
- Modeler
- Crayon Artist
- Portrait Painter
- Decorative Artist
- Musician { Vocal / Instrum'l
- Landscape Painter
- Dressmaker
- Tailor
- Milliner

COMMERCIAL
- Art Goods
- Musical Instruments
- Dry Goods
- Drugs
- Coal
- Clothing
- Flowers
- Speculation
- Real Estate
- Insurance
- Publishing
- Banking
- Hardware
- Boots and Shoes
- Jewelry
- Confectionery
- Books
- Lumber
- Produce
- Brokerage
- Commission
- Fancy Articles

EDUCATIONAL
- School Teacher
- Music Teacher
- Kindergarten Teach'r
- Teacher of Elocution
- Principal of Schools
- Teacher of Art
- Te'r of Penmanship
- Medical Lecturer
- Teacher of Language
- Teacher of Literature
- Teacher of Science

LITERARY
- Author
- Editor
- Elocutionist
- Librarian
- Lawyer
- Orator
- Reporter
- Poet
- Linguist
- Preacher
- Novelist
- Secretary
- Historian
- Actor
- Correspondent

MECHANICAL
- Jeweler
- Architect
- Blacksmith
- Cabinet Maker
- Contractor
- Machinist
- Printer
- Ship Builder
- Plumber
- Moulder
- Engraver
- Inventor
- Engin-eer { Civil / Electrical / Mechanical / Locomotive
- Finisher
- Carriage Maker
- Electrician
- Miller
- Carpenter
- Turner

SCIENTIFIC
- Surveyor
- Naturalist
- Mineralogist
- Physician
- Phrenologist
- Chemist
- Assayer
- Occulist
- Surgeon
- Dentist
- Geologist
- Aurist
- Botanist
- Anatomist
- Geographer
- Astronomer
- Microscopist
- Optician

MISCELLANEOUS
- Housekeeper
- Statesman
- Collector
- Agent
- Manager
- Farmer
- Stock Raiser
- Manufacturer
- Nurseryman
- Politician
- Professional Nurse
- Seaman
- Negotiator
- Poultryman
- Superintendent
- Hotel Keeper
- Fruit Grower
- Detective
- Organizer
- Salesman

CLERICAL
- Bookkeeper
- Stenographer
- Clerk
- Cashier
- Auditor
- Telegrapher

INDEX.

A.

Affection............... 32
Awkwardness............ 48
A great problem solved.... 59
Approbativeness — Back
  view 64
Argumentative disposition. 65
Activity................ 100
Acquisitiveness....100–103–170
Amativeness............. 97
Avarice................ 103
Altruism............... 117
A poor money saver...... 117
Abbott, Rev. Lyman...... 121
Ambition............ 122
A child genius......... 122
Agreeableness........... 129
Affectation............ 118
Accommodating.......... 164
Absentmindedness....... 146
Aristocracy 174
Aspiration............. 174
An intellectual wedge 198

B.

Bigamy 29
Bell, Prof. A. Graham..... 36
Brutality.............42–43
Blushing 52
Borrowing trouble....... 149
Bashfulness 149
Broad heads—The character
  of 106–107
Beauty 130
Boastfulness 164
Bluffing 197

C.

Conscientiousness 13
Concentration 19
Cooley, Judge Thomas Mc-
  Intyre 17

Crying—Another kind of... 25
Cruel eyes.............. 43
Caste 52
Changeableness 64
Curiosity 71
Child nature—Specific kinds
  of 82
Courage 84–152
Clumsy 85
Cheerfulness 95
Conservatism 120
Cautiousness 131
Character reading—A fun-
  damental system of. 137–138
Cowardice 149
Character in gesture...... 153
Combativeness 181
Constructiveness 180
Character in action........ 169
Centers of character....... 202
Character—The heart of... 9
Crying faculties 186
Credulity............... 206
Character in walking......
          211–212–213–214–215
Character in voice 222

D.

Deceitfulness 11
Deceitful features 14
Deceitful ear............ 16
Deceitful nose 153
Dangerous elements 38
Destructiveness 39
Disagreeableness 59
Desires 100
Disposition to crow....... 68
Diagnose your own case ..74–75
Domestic nature 79
Domineering disposition... 83
Divine—Human—Animal. 113

Defective Firmness 120
Dangerously incompetent. . 122
Danger....... 37-42
Don't 184
Dealing with yourself 246

E.

Energy—All the signs of... 41
Energy 45
Ears 62-133
Edison, Thomas A 70-71
Executive talent 99
Eyes and Head....125-126-127
Energetic divisions of the
  mind 137
Eye shutters..........183-184
Efficiency 181
Easily influenced......... 32
Elements and structure of
  will.................. 200
Eye openers..........185-186
Easily upset 224
Eyes 224-225
Especially watch the top-
  head 238
Elemental faculties de-
  fined.........239-240-241

F.

Feminine head and face ... 21
Father—A genuine 26
Father—An unreliable.... 27
Frivolity 41
Fitful.................. 64
Flirtation 78
Five centers 78
Folly 93
Fishing—The human na-
  ture of 107-108
Fear................... 114
Forceful resistance........ 118
Fanaticism 145
Friendship 177
Faculties that hold the body
  up................... 182
Force of character........ 188
Firmness in head and face.. 230
Framework of human char-
  acter 233

G.

Good child—How to pick
  out a 31
Greed................. 49
Gray, Elisha............ 69
Games 93
Genius 122
Gossiping 134
Gambling 153
Gullibility 157
Goodness............86-231
Get out 193
Get right at it........... 203
Gratitude 187
George, Henry 140

H.

Honesty 10
Honesty—A standard of.. 17
Honesty—All the signs of.. 19
Honest face............. 12
Honest features 15
Hospitality 13
Husband—A genuine 28
Husband—An unreliable .. 29
How to lead children...... 33
Howe, Julia Ward 35
Hesitation 149
Headwork 54
Humanitarianism 93
Human attraction.......
 108-109-156-157
Heaven—Earth—Hell 112
Hunting 135
How to read the nose 144
Handiwork 145
Heads and bodies......... 151
How to detect a friendly
  person 177-178
How character outs 162
Human Goodness......160-161
Hypnotic power.......... 34
Homesickness........... 134
Holy smoke 201
Harp of forty-two strings.. 163
How some of the faculties
  affect the body 196
High time to be definite ... 9
How to raise hair......... 187
How to read the face...204-205

Headwork 220
How can one be quick?.... 223
How much? 225
How we get rattled 229
How some of the faculties
   write 216-217

I.

Insincerity 16
Impressibility............ 31
Idiocy—Social 34
Impulsiveness 63–64
Individualism............ 81
Idealism 96–97
Intemperance 98
Infidelity................ 114
Intensity 119
Idiocy—Human......123–124
Intuition 130
Ignorance—A sign of..... 146
Inventive genius—The cen-
   ter of 180
Incredulity 170
Irritability 75
Individuality—Weak devel-
   opment of 197
Individuality—Strong de-
   velopment of 196
Instructive comparisons... 206
Intellectual hatchet....209–210
Instruction in locating the
   faculties 243–244–245

J.

Jealousy................. 134

K.

Keynote of a genius...... 190
Kindt, Gustave—Burglar
   and toolmaker........ 18

L.

Liars.................... 238
Love 30
Love of mischief 76
Love of the occult 113
Looker.................. 47
Lips 85–195
Longevity 93
Latent talent 94
Localization 223–242
Look for faculties 232
Look aright 111

M.

Masculine head and face.. 20
Masculine and feminine
   forms 22
Masculinity and Femininity 23
Mother—A genuine....... 24
Mother love 24
Mother—An unreliable.... 25
Military nature 43
Moods 43
Materialistic 91
Minor keys or faculties.... 104
Major keys or faculties.... 105
Modesty 129
Moody, D. L. 137
Mixed heads and faces....
  154–155–156
Musical genius 139
Marvelous 150
Mimicry 227
Mental inventory.....249–250

N.

Nervousness 51–52–216
Noses 9–80–89–221
Neatness 164
No escape 193

O.

Our spiritual eyes..... 158–159

P.

Prejudice 28
Polygamy 29
Pugnacity 37
Profanity 39–40
Pluck 50
Press the right button..... 54
Pugilism 58
Personal magnetism 65
Physical charms.......... 65
Pessimism 80
Personality—The center of 81
Psychical sensibility 90
Psychic phenomena—The
   center of............. 101
Pretension 73
Procrastination 131
Pointers 136
Patience 138
People whom animals love. 144
Psychological railway..171–172
Proud character.,....... 194

Practicability 173
Pointed points about char-
    acter reading 220
Ports of entry on the sea of
    life 251

R.

Reliability 199
Revenge 40–41
Rattles 64
Religiousness 68
Radicalism 102
Reticence 164
Reason 150
Representatives of indivi-
    dual faculties 237–238

S.

Slovenliness 25
Signs of love—All the 31
Savageism................. 43
Sensual chin.............. 43
Sensuality................ 44
Student—The thinking.... 46
Student—The visual....... 47
Self-esteem 83
Stubbornness 85
Skull 87–88
Sullenness 93
Socialism................. 117
Selfish territory 128–178
Susceptibility to in-
    sanity 132–133
Superstition 146
Selfishness—All the signs of 159
Stevenson, Robert Louis190–191
Secretiveness 179
Steadiness 172
Social evil,—The center of
    the 60–61
Suit the gesture to the fac-
    ulty 202
Self-esteem—Location of .. 182
Student—The auditory.... 195
Self-esteem—Negative 188
Selection of employees 225
Scale—A natural. 234–235–236
Stockton, Frank R........ 189

T.

Thinker 46
Two dangerous faculties... 77
Temperament.............. 94
Temper 72
The Torrid Zone......110–111
The Corn Faculty.....115–116
Trusts—The human nature
    of 128
Two outlines.........129–175
Teasing 136
Trinity of traitors 141–142
Theoretical 195
Thought centers.......192–193
Three principles.......... 234
Ten selfish faculties...... 226

U.

Underhandedness 13
Unsteadiness 135
Utility of bald heads...... 221

V.

Vanity 53–54
Vital magnetism 66
Vital magnetism—deficient 67
Veneration 86
Vital dynamo............. 95
Vitality 143–228

W.

Which touches the line?. 55–56
Well balanced head....... 57
Where to look.........80–226
Why some boys cannot raise
    a mustache 111
What makes people slow.. 124
Will—Taste—Feeling..... 132
Who are suspicious 138
Where the presidential bee
    buzzes 152
What two pictures tell. 167–168
Why Santa comes.....165–166
What the forty-two facul-
    ties do 194
What makes one handy... 173
Where voices come from... 218
While asleep............. 219
When you get tired flopping
    round................ 225
Wayward children........ 226

CPSIA information can be obtained
at www.ICGtesting.com
Printed in the USA
LVOW05s2245100217
523933LV00026B/602/P